...Just Another Day in the FBI...

Autumn Lynn & Jonathan

...Just Another Day in the FBI...

Best regards!!

Tony Oldham

Anthony E. Oldham

Copyright © 2016 Anthony E. Oldham
ISBN: 1537662376
ISBN: 9781537662374
Library of Congress Control Number: 2016915731
CreateSpace Independent Publishing Platform
North Charleston, South Carolina

The material in this book relates to actual incidents that occurred while I was employed by the Federal Bureau of Investigation (FBI). References to real people, events, establishments, organizations, or localities are factual and accurate as best that memory and research serve me. Many names are genuine, but in some instances, fictitious names are used to protect sources and operatives. Any resemblance to other actual events by use of these fictitious names or persons, living or dead, is entirely coincidental. This book is not an official publication of the FBI. Any opinions or views expressed in this book are those of the author and do not necessarily represent the opinions or views of the FBI or CreateSpace. Permission for the use of sources and graphics is solely the responsibility of the author.

Contents

Acknowledgments · vii

Terms · ix

Introduction · xi

Preface · xvii

Chapter 1   Bank Robberies · 1

Chapter 2   Fugitives · 59

Chapter 3   Kidnappings · 122

Chapter 4   Crisis Negotiations · 139

Chapter 5   Confidential Sources · · · · · · · · · · · · · · · · · · · 168

Chapter 6   Miscellaneous Duties · · · · · · · · · · · · · · · · · · · 182

Chapter 7   Memories · 224

Acknowledgments

———

I COULD NOT HAVE WRITTEN this book without the encouragement of my wife, Rosie, who has always stood behind me in any endeavor I have ever tried—except for golf, but that is another story for another day. Having been married for over fifty years, we have gone through all the trials and tribulations that any married couple could endure. Raising our four children, all boys—Brian, Kevin, Steven, and Kenneth—was a joy in itself but a trial for her when I left town for extended periods of time because of my job. Nevertheless, she persisted, and so did they. To this day, I can honestly say we accomplished all we wanted and more. Thank all of you for being there.

There is my brother, David, who was seven years younger than I and who followed me into the FBI as a special agent (SA), only to retire and be taken from all of us by brain cancer. He fought a valiant fight to the end. He was one fantastic baseball player as a youngster and later was the catcher for the New Mexico State University baseball team for four years. He even had an offer to play AAA ball for the Albuquerque Dukes (the LA Dodger organization) but chose to finish his education and subsequently went to work for the FBI. RIP and God be with you forever.

There is also my sister, Sharon, and her husband, Dave, who make sure I keep in touch with them and never stray too far away. Both have always stood behind me and Dave, who has joined my parents, Mary and James, both deceased.

A big thank you to all the employees of CreateSpace who helped turn my manuscript into final book form. A special thanks goes to Andrea, CreateSpace Editor who edited the entire manuscript and made an untold number of comments and suggestions to make this book read more interesting and professional. Your assistance was invaluable.

There are no sufficient words to describe my appreciation for all the SAs and support personnel in the FBI who keep this country safe for the American people. I often think back to my days years ago when we all worked together to get the job done. We never looked at each other as extraordinary in any way but just as a group of dedicated Americans tasked to do the job at hand and working to accomplish expected goals.

Many detractors demean the good people of the FBI, but there are many more who respect us and understand what difficult jobs we have. We all have our faults and failures simply because we are human, but we will never shirk our responsibilities, because of our sworn promise to protect and defend the Constitution of this great country, the United States of America.

A huge thank-you goes out to all my friends who listened to some of my work-related incidents and encouraged me to write this book. They promised that if I did, they would buy it. That was enough for me. So here it is—open your wallets.

Terms

———

THERE ARE MANY ABBREVIATED TERMS used in this book, and this page will help you identify them.

ABA............................ Arizona Bar Association
APB............................. All-points bulletin
ASAC .... Assistant special agent in charge
AUSA........................... Assistant US attorney
BOLO .... Be on lookout
BR............................... Bank robbery
BUCAR .... Official FBI vehicle
CI .... Criminal informant
DMV............................ Department of Motor Vehicles
DOJ............................. Department of Justice
DPS .... Department of Public Safety
FBI .... Federal Bureau of Investigation
FBIHQ .... Federal Bureau of Investigation
                                         headquarters
FGJ.............................. Federal grand jury
FOA............................. First office agent
HRT .... Hostage rescue team
IO .... Identification order

MCSO .... Maricopa County Sheriff's Office
PXPD........................... Phoenix Police Department
RA .... Resident agency
SA .... Special Agent
SAC .... Special agent in charge
SAS............................. Special air services
SBS.............................. Special boat services
SPD .... Scottsdale Police Department
UFAP........................... Unlawful flight to avoid prosecution
USMC .... United States Marine Corps

Introduction

———

On Friday, September 29, 1995, I worked my last day with the FBI, retiring out of the Phoenix division after serving twenty-seven and a half years with this great organization. I had put in my retirement papers several months earlier after giving it much thought, recognizing that I was not getting any younger, that I had spent my entire adult life in law enforcement, and that life had other things to offer. Don't get me wrong—the career I chose was very fulfilling, giving me memories of a lifetime and taking me to physical and mental places I had never dreamed of going.

On the evening of my retirement, I enjoyed a party put on by my lovely wife, Rosie, with the help of the local FBI office and some friends and colleagues. It was a night I will never forget.

On the following Monday morning, I slept in late, rising at 5:30 a.m. When I was working, I rose at about 3:30 a.m. or 4:00 a.m., showered, and drove to the office, arriving at about 4:30 a.m. or 5:00 a.m. Although coming to the office early in the morning, I was not the first one there. SA Al Zumph, a colleague and very good friend of mine, was always ahead of me.

I missed the rush-hour traffic by leaving the house so early and was able to make telephone calls to the FBI offices located in the eastern part of the United States before the personnel left their respective offices for investigations they might be conducting. Also, as I was working on a fugitive task force called Desert Hawk, many times an early-morning contact at a residence allowed us to find the fugitive we were seeking to arrest. My day usually ended at around 6:30 p.m., if I was lucky. The hours were long, but the days always seemed too short. As the old saying goes, if it's fun, it's not a job.

But that Monday morning was very unusual. I knew this was the first day I did not have to go to work, and the pressure I had felt over the years was nonexistent. I had never even realized the pressure I was under until the day I no longer had it. What a change this was. Instead of deciding to assault a residence to find a fugitive, I now had to decide what time I was leaving to play golf. This was a great feeling. However, I also knew that it might take me some time to adjust to this new way of life, and I certainly was not wrong about that.

I must admit that whenever I heard that the FBI had made an arrest, the old adrenaline rush came and made me feel that perhaps I had left my career too early, that my retiring had been premature.

One evening about two weeks after retirement, I came home after a round of golf, several hours at the clubhouse drinking beer with golf partners, and then a few hands of gin, recognizing there was more to that silly game than just looking at cards and hoping for the best. It cost me a few coins to learn the game, and it was fun. But I digress.

When I got home, I turned on the television, and there was a news helicopter flying over a taped-off crime scene several miles from where

I lived. I noticed several cars in an intersection that appeared to have collided with one another. Then a close-up shot showed a person on a phone, and that person was Danny Snodgrass, a Phoenix police detective assigned to our fugitive task force. Apparently, our fugitive team was involved in an arrest. Knowing Danny's cell number, I waited a bit and then called him and watched him answer the phone on TV, given the seven- or ten-second delay that the media has to make sure you do not see an actual event occur that might upset you. Danny told me that they had finally found a fugitive we had been looking for just before I had retired. They saw him driving a car and tried to arrest him after blocking his car with other police and FBI vehicles. He pulled out a gun and pointed it at our team. Big mistake. Our team was well trained, and when he did that, Danny and others fired at him, striking and killing him instantly. I got the usual adrenaline rush I used to experience and wished I was back in the action with them.

He suggested I come down to see all the guys as they would be there for a while, but I declined. I told him that I needed to accept the fact that I was retired and not keep wondering if I had done the right thing. Eventually, I came to the conclusion that I had made the correct decision and never looked back again.

I noticed that since the day I retired and over the many years to this day, I would meet many new people. The majority of the time, once they learned I previously worked for the FBI, they showed a renewed interest in carrying on a conversation. They always asked in what part of the country I worked, if I knew a particular SA they had known years ago, and what I did in the FBI. Apparently, the FBI carries a prestigious aura, and people wanted to know what it was like to be an SA. I would tell them, and eventually it got to where people would ask me to tell them about a case or two, and I would comply.

As time went on, my closest friends told me that I should write a book because of all the experiences I had, but to me and other SAs, the work we did was great but did not seem unusual. It was just another day of work for all of us. The idea of writing a book intrigued me, but I never got around to it. I decided, however, to put some of my experiences down on paper, so when that final day came, and I hopefully would be going down that road to salvation, my grandchildren would have a record of what I did. So I compiled notes and put them aside.

I finally decided to put this in the form of a book, and this is what you have in your hands. When deciding what to name the book, I thought it was prudent to call it ...*Just Another Day in the FBI*... because that explains the mind-set of many SAs. We do not think of ourselves as anything special (although when working with the FBI, we are referred to as *Special Agents*) but just a dedicated group of men and women who seek to find justice on behalf of the American people. We love what we do, want no extraordinary accolades, and hope to retire with the knowledge that we never abandoned our fidelity, bravery, and integrity, the three words that form FBI.

Let me state right here that all the solved cases in this book were because of the combined efforts of many SAs, support personnel, detectives from local agencies and other federal agencies, and many others, including confidential sources and the general public. I only tell these stories to explain my objective point of view and what I was doing at the time to help others solve cases and accomplish our goals. I am not the lone factor in these resolutions but just one of many. I do not claim to be the best the FBI had to offer but just one man trying to do my part to maintain the respect and integrity the FBI has generated over the years. So if it sounds as if I boast a bit, please understand that it is because of the people I worked with over the years who gave me the opportunity to accomplish my objectives and successes, and I am proud of that.

I hope you enjoy reading about the experiences I encountered in real life. I did not embellish nor downplay anything in this book. Some names are authentic, and some are fictitious, depending on the circumstances or memory lapses. Everything written came from my personal memory as best as I can recall, and little research was done, although some was done to refresh my memory as to names and dates of individual events. However, my primary objective was to describe these stories from my perceptions as they occurred.

Some cases are funny, some are sad, some are dramatic, and some are mundane. But they are all actual cases. I sincerely hope you enjoy reading about them as much as I have enjoyed relating them to you.

Author Anthony E. Oldham many years ago.

Preface

———

ON A VERY CHILLY EARLY afternoon, the neatly dressed man strolled quite casually through the main entrance of the bus station so as to not draw any attention and proceeded to the check-in counter. The terminal was rather quiet at that time of day, and there was a very short line to stand in before he approached the female ticket agent with the ticket he had earlier purchased. She checked him in as he proceeded to check the one bag he was taking as he left a town to which he planned never to return. He held on to his carry-on bag to take it with him on the bus. It was November 1967, and other people were arriving to check in and catch their buses or meet loved ones who were coming into town.

After completing the check-in process, he turned to walk toward the departure door, when he noticed the same two men he had seen earlier as he arrived at the bus station. They started to follow him casually, so he picked up his pace a bit, watching them out of the corner of his eye. He noticed that they both picked up their pace as well. As he hurried forward, he observed several other men in suits approaching him from the front and knew that his time was short unless he could evade all of them.

Just then he heard one of the men yell, "Mitchell, stop. FBI. We need to talk to you." Mitchell started to run in a different direction to avoid them, and as he did, he reached into his carry-on bag and retrieved a gun he'd placed there after robbing a local bank earlier that day. After the robbery, he had returned to his motel room to change clothes, donning a business suit and packing his suitcase so he could leave town. He had plenty of time before his bus was to leave, but he still had to return the car he'd rented when he had arrived in town several days prior.

Just as he gripped the gun and drew it out of the bag, one of the men again yelled, "FBI. Drop the gun!" There was no way he was going back to prison, so he raised the weapon and pointed it at the FBI agents, and several shots rang out.

Just then the motel doorbell rang, indicating that a customer had entered the lobby. My wife, Rosie, asked me if I could take care of the new customer. Damn, I thought. I'm going to miss the end of this show. I knew that Efrem Zimbalist Jr., or Mr. FBI, would get his man, but I would not see it happen. I had to leave the TV set and serve the customer who came into the Ambassador Motel, which my wife and I managed for her uncle in Gallup, New Mexico, the town where I was born and raised. Nevertheless, I still managed to get a peek through the crack of the door to see the subject being arrested and attended to for the wounds received in the shootout. I proceeded to the business at hand and rented out a room to the traveler, who was coming from California with his family for some destination farther east. I directed him to his room and then returned to the television hoping to see the ending of the show. I was able to see a one-minute commercial followed by a familiar weekly concluding scene showing a car driven out of the confines of the Justice Department building in Washington, DC. The one-hour presentation of *The FBI* was over for the week. Inspector Lewis Erskine had gotten his man again.

Well, it was getting a bit late, so I made my final checks of the motel complex, finished the necessary bookwork, and locked the lobby door but kept the vacancy sign on in the event that some late traveler might come looking for a room sometime during the night. Business was always slow during these winter months, so we made sure to get all the business we could whenever we could.

Plus I had to get to bed so that I could wake up at 5:30 a.m., get a lunch packed, and drive out to a construction site where I worked as a labor supervisor for my dad, who had a construction company. I had to make sure that there was sufficient brick or block available and cement mixed so that the bricklayers would start to work promptly at 8:00 a.m. Construction was a serious business, and any wasted time lost money, so it was unacceptable for bricklayers to be standing around while the hod carriers were stocking up and mixing cement.

It sure was cold on those winter mornings, so a good, warm fire was started once I got to the job site, both for warmth and to melt the ice that had formed in the large barrels holding water used to mix the cement. After work was completed that day at 4:30 p.m., I returned home to the motel, cleaned up, ate the good food (mostly lasagna) that Rosie always made for me, and began another evening of renting rooms to travelers. The motel business was an intense, work-infested atmosphere, but the additional money from managing this business was good and helped now that we'd just had our first child. Also, we lived on site at this motel and were not charged rent, so that was a real plus.

I had become interested in the FBI at a younger age but never actually considered pursuing that goal, believing it was far beyond my reach. It was a point of interest, but as I grew, I did what most other typical teenagers did: went to school, played sports, dated, danced, and met up with others at the local hamburger drive-in—in this case, a hangout named Lori's. As I got older and graduated from high school in 1963, I started working at the local telephone company, spending three years there as a telephone installer and central-office technician as well as plant-line assigner and framer. This central-office assignment was excellent, especially in the winter, when it was terribly cold outside. I married my high-school sweetheart, Rosie Knight, in 1965 and became a volunteer firefighter in this small town of seventeen thousand people. I bought a brand-new car from the factory, ordered to my specifications, and became the proud owner of a 1965 Pontiac GTO, burgundy with white interior, 389 cubic inches with three two-barrel carburetors and four on the floor. My new GTO was the first that ever graced the streets of Gallup, New Mexico. I did this all for $3,600, a pretty pricey amount for a car in those days. Life was good as I sped to a fire in this great-looking car that had a siren under the hood. Rosie thought I was going nuts, but as I said, life was good and could not have been better.

However, as time went on and the work got a bit annoying, going to fires became nothing but a small adventure, and there was not much good on the three TV channels we had. I played on several men's softball teams with my buddies, but I was getting bored with everything I was doing. I needed more adventure in my life, and I started seriously thinking about a change in careers. I liked the people in Gallup since many of them were good, hardworking individuals, and to this day I still see many of them. They all have a special place in my heart. But I believed that if I was going to find something more exciting in life, I would probably need a change of locale to find it.

My interest in the FBI piqued as I occasionally observed a tall, neatly dressed gentleman walking toward the local FBI field office located in the basement of the old post office. I learned that he was the newest FBI agent and a recent transfer to the Gallup resident agency (RA), and his name was Ken. This RA was a satellite office out of the Albuquerque division of the FBI, and the SAs assigned to this RA lived in the Gallup area and addressed all federal violations that occurred within this designated area. Ken always had the persona of a dignified individual representing a very professional agency. My daily thoughts turned to dreams of becoming an FBI SA. I hesitated mentioning this to Rosie as it was merely an idea at that point, and I wanted to get more information before I told her about it.

One day, I saw this new FBI SA walking toward the local mortuary, approached him, and introduced myself. I asked if there was a possibility that I could speak with him about an FBI career. He was very cordial, and as a result, we set up an appointment for the following day. I talked with him for a few minutes more and found out that he was one of two special agents (SAs) assigned to the Gallup resident agency.

The following day, I went down to the old post-office basement to the FBI office for this informal interview. I was admitted by the other SA assigned to this RA. He told me to take a seat and that Ken would be with me shortly. Ken was on the telephone with someone he was looking to arrest and was allowing this person to surrender to the FBI so that his family would not be watching his imminent arrest occur.

Once off the phone, Ken filled me in on the qualifications needed to become an FBI SA. I learned that I would need to return to college and obtain a four-year degree, preferably in accounting or law, but any college degree was acceptable as long as I was able to get at least three years' experience in the private sector specializing in that subject matter. Also, I would have a complete and thorough background check, and if I was successful in passing that, I would be eligible to take oral and written exams and a complete physical exam. I would have to agree to be transferred to any FBI field office in the United States or virtually anywhere in the world where the FBI had an interest. If I completed all these requirements, I would be put on a list and wait my turn to be selected for an SA appointment.

Oh, by the way, there were approximately twenty-five thousand eligible applicants on the list as we spoke. Everybody wanted to be a Special Agent of the FBI, and when I heard this large number, my hopes just went out the door.

It sure was a downer hearing this. How was I going to compete against all those others who were on the list waiting for an appointment? But I could not see myself working much longer for the telephone company and managing a motel to derive extra income. I was unsure what I wanted to do.

I made a decision and resigned from the phone company shortly after talking to Ken, knowing that as long as I was employed there, I would never leave. So I turned in my two-week notice and left. It was a difficult decision to make but one that I thought was important. My mom thought I was nuts, and my dad thought I was delusional. I was not happy working at the telephone company, so the decision came a bit more easily. Fortunately, I was able to go immediately to work for my dad in construction as I had formerly worked as a labor supervisor for him, and he needed someone to supervise some employees on a new job.

In fact, my dad wanted me to stay in Gallup and take over his construction business. I had been mixing cement and carrying block for him as a hod carrier since I was in the eighth grade, when he started me working for twenty-five cents an hour. But each year my pay increased by about fifty cents an hour. I was allowed to keep half that amount, and the rest went into a savings account to help pay for the seventy-five-dollar tuition fees and clothes for my sister, Sharon, and me at Cathedral High School. But I had my fill of concrete and sand. I was in good shape, well tanned, and young, but the construction field was not my idea of what I wanted as my career choice.

After getting this information about the FBI from Ken (who later rose through the ranks, retiring as a deputy assistant director, a highly responsible and respected position), I went home and talked to Rosie. She was a bit stunned as she did not want me running around chasing criminals and getting into shootouts. I told her that was all on TV, and she just rolled her eyes. She became concerned as I told her all the qualifications I needed, and she then thought that I had lost my mind. We discussed this for several days, and the more I talked, the more excited I got, and the less resistant she became. Finally, she said that I should chase my dream, even if it looked like something that might be out of reach. What a great gal, giving me such encouragement!

So in early 1968, we drove to Phoenix, Arizona. My plan was to register at Arizona State University to get my degree and pursue my goal. I visited a large electronics firm that was currently hiring and applied for work. My plans were to work full time and go to school part time until I obtained my degree. On a hunch, I went to the local FBI office in Phoenix and met with SA Ted Crowley, who gave me a tour of the office. He was just as enthusiastic as Ken and handed me a blank application to fill out. I thought, *Boy, these guys must really want me.* Little did I know that all SAs were tasked with locating and recruiting qualified applicants for employment, and Ted just happened to be the applicant coordinator for the

Phoenix division. I asked Ted if the possibility existed that I might be able to work for the FBI in Phoenix as I went to school at night, and he said he would find out. He told me to fill out the application form immediately in the event that I might be able to work in a clerical capacity until I obtained my college degree. So that evening at my sister's house, I filled out this incredibly lengthy application form and noted just about everything there was to know about my past life.

The following day, I took the completed application back to the FBI office, and SA Crowley told me that the local field office did not have any slots open at this time, but he could start the background investigation on me if I wanted him to. If I passed the background and a slot opened up, I could be considered for the clerical job. He said, however, that if I successfully passed the background and wanted to go to work immediately for the FBI, I could travel at my expense to Washington, DC, and work there in a clerical capacity as the FBI currently had openings in Washington.

Rosie and I again talked about it, and this sounded like a real adventure, so we decided to go ahead with the background investigation and see what developed. We knew it would be a real challenge, but it sounded interesting and exciting. We returned to Gallup to wait to see if anything would happen. Shortly, we knew that something was astir as my mom and dad were getting calls from friends and relatives saying that the FBI had been asking about me; being from a small town, they wanted to know what I had done to deserve such scrutiny. Of course, my folks were proud of my undertaking and told everyone I was going to work for the FBI even before I had received any appointment letter.

Shortly after that, I received a letter from the FBI that was signed by J. Edgar Hoover, offering me a clerical position in Washington, DC, with a starting salary of about $3,000 a year. It was not much money but enough for us to live on—we hoped. I was to report for assignment at the old post office building in Washington, DC, on March 4, 1968.

The rest is history. We moved to the DC area, and I worked at the FBI identification division doing fingerprint classification and identification for about four years. During this time, I occasionally gave tours at the Justice Department, where the FBI headquarters was located until the new FBI building was later built just across the street. I worked during the day and attended school at night at Southeastern University, a small business college, where I subsequently obtained my bachelor's degree in business administration. Because I had worked in a law-enforcement capacity for my four years at the FBI, I was afforded the opportunity to take the Special Agent entrance examination. I completed all the physicals, oral interviews, and written tests and received a Special Agent appointment date of May 8, 1972, for a new-agents class at Quantico, Virginia. Our class, number ten, was the very first one that opened the new FBI Academy at Quantico. I went through fourteen weeks of intensive training with forty-nine other SA hopefuls, striving to complete all the rigorous demands. On our last day of training, we were given our credentials and told to pick up our weapons at the armory and get the hell out of town and on to our new assignments. There were no ceremonies as there are today at Quantico, but we were excited and happy to complete training and get on with saving the world from all the criminals who were just waiting for us to show up. My first assignment was in Columbia, South Carolina, and Rosie and I were happy to be leaving the hectic pace of Washington, DC.

During this stint in Washington, we had had three more children, so Rosie, Brian, Kevin, Steven, Kenneth, and I all packed up and headed south for my new career. We stayed in Columbia for about two years, and I worked primarily all crimes that occurred at the Fort Jackson, South Carolina, military base; after that, I was transferred to Phoenix, Arizona, where I worked until I retired from the FBI in 1995. During this career, I was engaged in numerous investigations and arrests. There was adventure and boredom, grief and satisfaction, long hours, short days, and decent pay. But, more than anything, there were everlasting memories of events available only to a select few.

The events I describe in this book are all factual, and experienced by myself and others I worked with. I wanted to explain these cases in the most interesting way without embellishment or drama; the resolutions of the investigations are all factual, and therefore I will describe the events as I recall to the best of my memory. I decided that if there might be a case where the facts were questionable because of the lapse of time and no reference was available to obtain sufficient, accurate data, the case would not be published in this book.

As I recall and recount the memorable events as I pass through this book, I may refer to many of the criminals by fictitious names because, for the most part, these events happened years ago, and I cannot recall all of their names. Also, some of the law-enforcement personnel may be addressed by aliases to protect their identities. I use these names as source references to continue the flow of each incident as it occurred. I did not want to refer to the subjects as robbers, kidnappers, et cetera, but to personalize each with a name. Any factual reference to any one person is strictly unintentional or coincidental. Some are intentional.

Author at FBI Academy, Quantico, VA. circa 1972

Author at FBI Academy Firearms Range, Quantico, VA

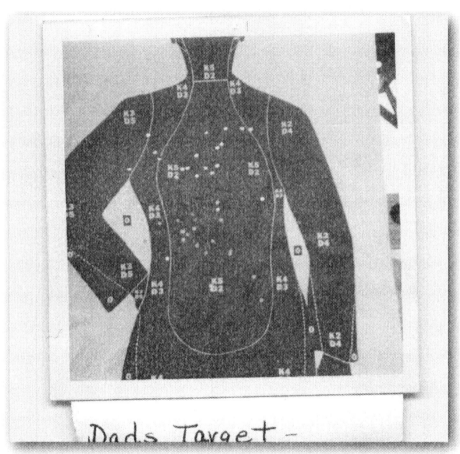

Shooting target - Hole between body and arm is a warning shot. I stand by that.

CHAPTER 1

Bank Robberies

——◆——

BANK-ROBBERY VIOLATIONS HAVE BEEN INVESTIGATED by the FBI and local authorities for decades. The FBI has jurisdiction to investigate these violations primarily because the federal government insures the assets of most banks, making this a federal violation. A robbed bank is also investigated by local authorities as they have concurrent jurisdiction with the FBI. As a rule, local officers, detectives, and federal agents will jointly work the robbery, with one of these agencies (federal, state, or local) assuming prosecutorial discretion. In other words, the robber could be prosecuted by the US Department of Justice, the state attorney general, or the local prosecutor.

Bank robberies are a major problem in the United States. When I was assigned to the Phoenix division, every year we could be confident that around 150 banks would be robbed in the State of Arizona. Some of these robberies would be committed by repeat offenders until they were identified, arrested, convicted, and confined in a federal or state correctional facility. The bank robbers got little money for the risk they took in committing the robberies, but the thieves just kept coming. Larger offices in California might have around nine hundred robberies yearly within the different California divisions.

Bank robberies are committed in several styles. The most prevalent involves robbers who come into the banks, produce a bank-robbery demand note, either claim to have or produce a weapon, take the money given from the victimized teller, and leave the bank with very few customers even knowing the bank has just been robbed. Then there are the take-down artists, who barge into a bank, loudly announce the robbery, put everyone down on the floor, and take the money from as many tellers as they can within a short period of time. These robbers usually work in larger groups and are very dangerous as it does not take much for them to discharge their weapons and possibly injure, if not, kill someone.

Regardless of the type of robbery, the FBI works these violations with a significant amount of manpower because of the dangerous nature of this crime. The robbers ran from the young to the old, can be either male or female, and come from different ethnic backgrounds. Here are a few of the robberies I investigated that you might find interesting.

Author with Special Agent Jason Deaton on the bank robbery squad

I was conducting leads one day on a previous case when the bank-robbery alarm came over my car radio, informing all SAs that a bank located on East Indian School Road had been robbed by a young white male wearing a white shirt and white pants. I proceeded to the bank and immediately joined other SAs who had arrived to conduct the investigation. Upon entering the bank, I noticed that the area where the robber had stood to get the money from the bank teller was roped off to prevent any outside contamination until the area was dusted for fingerprints and all evidence retrieved. This evidence protection was standard procedure at any crime scene, and as I approached the area, I noticed that the bank robber had left the demand note on the counter. Usually, robbers take the note with them when they exit the bank, but occasionally thieves will leave the note there. That way, the note will not be in their possession in the event that they are stopped by authorities after the robbery.

I glanced at the note, which contained a demand for money, nothing more than a typical bank-robbery demand. The robber had handed this note to the bank teller, who complied with the request and gave the robber the money he asked for. The teller had retained the note and left it on the counter after the robber left the bank. Careful not to contaminate any other evidence that might exist, I picked the note up and turned it over. I noticed that it was written on the back of a bank deposit slip of some customer. This deposit slip was not a counter slip that could be obtained at the bank but was the type that had the customer's name and address imprinted on it. Also, on the upper left corner, where the name and address were preprinted, the information was scratched out so as to obliterate the identifying information; however, it was scratched out with a pencil. I could not believe that any robber would use his own deposit slip to write a demand, but over the years, I came to the conclusion that bank robbers were not the smartest people walking this planet. I just took an eraser and erased the pencil markings to reveal the name of Robert Anderson and this person's address. Several other agents looked at this note, and we all laughed, not believing that this guy could be so dumb. It seemed a good lead to follow, so several of us left the bank and proceeded to the address noted on the slip.

Upon arrival at this address, located just a short distance from the bank, several of us went to the door to make an inquiry of the resident. A young man answered the door and gave us a name that was different from the one on the deposit slip/demand note. We asked him if he had any roommates, and he said that his roommate was now at work. He gave us his name, Bob Anderson. Lo and behold, Robert Anderson was the name printed on the deposit slip/demand note. He said his roommate worked at a fast-food restaurant but should be returning home shortly. He stated that Anderson wore a standard work uniform at this restaurant, described as a white shirt, white trousers, and a small white hat.

He provided a description of Anderson, which was similar to that of the robber. We did not want to tell this young man why we were looking for his roommate but mentioned that we just needed to ask him a few questions. He relaxed a bit, saying that Anderson was a decent person who had never been in any trouble in his entire life.

We told the young man that we would like to wait around, and he had no objection. Within approximately ten minutes, he looked out the window and said that his roommate was walking down the street and coming home. We went outside to meet him, and here was this young man in a white shirt, white pants, and white hat, carrying a white sandwich bag. He looked up at us and pretty much guessed who we were; he immediately held out the bag and said, "Here's the money." Case solved.

Unfortunately, Anderson was stressed out with the rigors of life that we all go through and felt the only way to catch up on his bills was to rob a bank—not the smartest thing to do, especially when he used his own deposit slip to write the demand. He was arrested and charged with bank robbery and later entered a guilty plea after the assistant US attorney (AUSA) and the defense attorney agreed on a settlement. There was no loss of money from the bank as the recovered money from Anderson was immediately returned. Anderson was young, had never been in any serious trouble, admitted to the robbery, and was remorseful for what he had done. Therefore, he was subsequently sentenced to serve a short jail term—an extremely fortunate outcome for him as the maximum duration for bank robbery is twenty years in a federal penitentiary.

———◆———

Years later, I worked another bank robbery with very similar results. Upon entering the bank following the robbery, I noticed that the demand note was on the counter. When I turned over the plain piece of paper, I saw a small yellow sticky note stuck to it. Written on this yellow paper were a first name and a telephone number.

During this robbery, a surveillance camera was activated and captured several photographs of the robber. Copies of this photo were made and distributed to investigators and police officers in the vicinity of the bank. A Phoenix police officer saw the photograph and thought he had stopped this same person several days earlier to speak with him since he appeared to be a vagrant and was loitering near some businesses, generating a complaint from a particular business. At that time, the officer had taken his name and other identifying data and told him to move on or he would be arrested for loitering and creating a disturbance. The officer said he would try to find the person's name in his log book and let us know once he found it.

Meanwhile, I called the telephone number on the yellow sticky paper, and when the phone was answered, I was stunned to learn that it was the phone number of the parole board in downtown Phoenix. I asked for the person whose name appeared on the note, and when I talked to that person, I explained to him what had occurred. He advised that he handled many, many parolees and usually gave them a card with his name and telephone number on it, so they could contact him as directed. He did say, however, that he had one parolee to whom he had recently verbally given his phone number over the telephone, and he provided me with that person's name and address. He described this person to me, and this description met the one of the bank robber. He further said that this man had been released from jail recently, suffered from depression and alcoholism, and was living with his father in the northwest Phoenix area. The father's residence was a short distance from the bank that was robbed.

Shortly after I obtained this information, the police officer returned to the bank and gave us the name of the vagrant he had confronted several days earlier. It was the same name given to us by the parole officer.

Several SAs and detectives went to the given address and talked with the father, who told us that when he had seen his son several hours earlier, he was drinking heavily and said that he was going to get a motel room for the night. However, he did not tell his father which motel he would be going to. Figuring that since he did not have a car, he would not be going too far away, we started going to all the nearby motels in the area, armed with the photograph that he had. Within one hour, we had taken the subject into custody but had recovered very little money taken from the bank. Shortly after the robbery, he had purchased a cowboy shirt, Levi's, boots, and a bottle of whiskey. He confessed to the robbery, and we had another case solved. It was just another stupid mistake of a desperate person, who was convicted of this robbery and subsequently returned to prison.

———————

Late one Friday afternoon in north Phoenix, a bank was robbed by a lone white male who was seen driving westbound in an older brown or rust-colored car. The witness could not say what make of car it was but reported that it was older and sort of beaten up. Several agents had gone to the bank and said there were very few witnesses to interview, so several of us proceeded westbound from the bank, checking parking lots and apartment complexes for this older car.

Approximately forty-five minutes later, several of us found a car meeting the description; it was parked in a space at an apartment complex. We requested a search from the Arizona Department of Motor Vehicles (DMV) for ownership of this car based on the license plate. The parking space was identified, and we learned from a maintenance man which apartment it belonged to. We went upstairs to the apartment and confronted several young men, many of whom met the description we had of the robber. The description given to us by witnesses was very vague and did not help us at all. I asked the group of young men who owned the car in the designated space, and one of them mentioned that he was in the process of purchasing it. He gave me his name as Scott Baker and this did not match the name we had from our record check at the DMV since he was just buying the car, and it had not officially changed ownership. I asked Baker if he had any objection to allowing us to search the car because it matched the description of one used in a bank robbery. He said he had no objection, so I had him sign a consent form, and we searched the car.

We did not find any evidence, but we did find a small amount of marijuana residue, which was not unusual, and some other drug paraphernalia. However, in the backseat, there was a black baseball cap with a unique and distinctive name imprinted on the front. It was a hard-to-pronounce word, possibly foreign, of about fourteen letters. It was quite distinctive, unusual, and singular in nature. In other words, it stood out. What also made this so interesting was that a week earlier, another bank had been robbed by a young white male wearing a hat with this same name on it, and that bank was not far from that apartment complex. We had a surveillance photograph of that robber; his face was concealed by the brim of the hat, but the photo displayed a great view of the cap.

As we conducted the search of this vehicle, several other agents interviewed all these young men separately. The SAs found that they were getting conflicting statements when all the gathered information was compared. However, all the young men had denied any knowledge of the bank robbery that had just occurred. I contacted the US Attorney's Office and spoke with an AUSA, giving him the information of this day's robbery as well as the facts of the robbery a week earlier, including the hat we had just located. The AUSA authorized prosecution, and we arrested Scott Baker, who was purchasing the car and who earlier claimed ownership of the black ball cap.

As I advised Baker that he was under arrest for bank robbery, I started to inform him of his constitutional rights under the Miranda rule. These are the same rights given by authorities to a suspect after arrest if an interview is to take place. As I was doing so, one of his buddies started yelling at me and telling Baker that he did not have to talk to me. I told him to back off and again started the Miranda rights, all the while listening to the other person telling Baker not to speak to me.

I had finally had enough of this loudmouth. I walked over and told him that I needed his name. He asked me why, and I merely said that I needed it to determine if he was an attorney and was a member of the Arizona Bar Association (ABA). He looked stunned, so I told him that he had been giving legal advice to his friend, so he must be an attorney. If he was not, I needed to turn his name over to the ABA for disciplinary action as the ABA does not take kindly to people practicing law without a license. Another SA standing nearby heard me, agreed, and told me that he would contact the ABA immediately to confirm him as an attorney. The young man said that he was not an attorney, and I asked the other SA if we should arrest him. The SA said that if the young man quieted down, we might let this pass. The young man turned and went into the apartment, and we never observed him again that evening. Fortunately, this clown had no clue that we were using a ruse on him just to quiet him down. To this date, I cannot be certain if he still believes what we were telling him—but, young man, if you are reading this, relax—you did nothing wrong other than being a jerk. Oh, I suppose we could have arrested him for obstruction of justice if he kept it up, but we did not have the time or inclination to do so. We just wanted to complete our investigation and arrest those responsible for robbing the bank.

This case subsequently went to trial, and along with additional evidence that we obtained through a further investigation, we convicted Baker on both counts of bank robbery. However, the case was appealed to the Ninth Circuit in San Francisco, and the convictions were overturned. The Ninth Circuit advised that in its judicial opinion, the agent (me) had failed to warn the subjects of their constitutional right of self-incrimination when I first confronted them and attempted to determine ownership of the vehicle parked in the space at the apartment complex. I found this to be interesting since all I was trying to do at that time was determine the genuine and correct identity of the owner of the car, so I could seek permission to search the vehicle through consent. I was just conducting the investigation and at that time had no intention of arresting anyone as we did not know for certain if this vehicle was the one used in the robbery. Therefore, I had not been mandated by law to advise anyone of their Miranda rights concerning self-incrimination. I had followed all legal procedures appropriately, and I still believe that the Ninth Circuit was incorrect in its finding. In fact, one of the judges on the court agreed that I did not need to advise anyone of the rights not to self-incriminate at that time. Baker had been later informed of his Miranda rights once I determined him to be the subject of the case and was preparing to arrest him and interview him. But the Ninth Circuit's decision stood.

The AUSA who prosecuted the case was furious with the decision and decided to retry Baker again for both bank robberies. Baker and his attorney contacted the AUSA and advised that if the government did not retry the defendant, Baker would enter a guilty plea to one count of bank robbery. The AUSA asked me what I thought, and I had no objection as I had other things to do besides sit through another trial. Baker entered a guilty plea to the one count and was sentenced to prison, and I went on with my life. Case(s) solved.

———

I had just transferred to the Phoenix division in 1974 and was working white-collar crime cases. Anytime a bank robbery occurred in the division, all SAs were expected to respond and assist the SAs who were on the bank-robbery squad. Bank robberies were violent crimes and, on many occasions, necessitated an immediate response to identify, locate, and apprehend the robber before anyone was harmed or killed. Unfortunately, once a thief robbed a bank and was successful, he or she determined it was easy money and would often try again until captured. However, it was a stupid crime as the robber would get maybe a couple of thousand dollars and risked up to twenty years in prison if apprehended. That term could be twenty-five years if a weapon was used. The more robberies committed by one person, the more likelihood he or she would be apprehended and receive substantial time in prison.

A radio transmission from the FBI office notified all units that a bank robbery had just occurred in Glendale, Arizona, and the dispatcher provided the location of the bank and the description of the robber. He was a middle-aged Hispanic, about five feet, eight inches tall, wearing a blue shirt and Levi's. The money had been placed in a paper bag, and the robber had been last seen leaving the bank and walking fast in an eastbound direction.

I was still trying to get my bearings around Phoenix and the surrounding suburbs, so I pulled out my local map, got a rough idea of where this bank was located, and proceeded to drive to Glendale to work the robbery. It took me about twenty-five minutes to get to the Glendale area from Phoenix, and as I was driving, the dispatcher advised that there were very few witnesses to be interviewed as other SAs were already at the bank, interviewing them. All other SAs could proceed to the area and look for the robber if he was on foot. However, if he had a car parked away from the bank, he would be long gone.

I was not too far, so I asked the dispatcher if Glendale had a bus station, and she affirmed that there was one and gave me the location. Coincidentally, I was approaching the bus station at that same time and told her that I would be stopping by to see if the robber might have gone there and left the area by bus. It was a long shot but a lead nevertheless.

I parked by Bucar, took my portable radio, and entered the station. As I did, I looked toward the benches to my left to see if anyone sitting there met the description of the robber. There were very few people waiting for a bus, but in the very last row of benches, a lone middle-aged Hispanic male wearing a blue shirt was sitting quietly. I turned to the counter to my right, identified myself to the ticket agent on duty, and said that I was going to talk to the person in the last row and that I wanted him to call the Glendale Police Department for backup if I alerted him. It was probably nothing, but I just wanted to confirm this for myself.

I walked to where this person was sitting and watched his eyes turn toward the wall to avoid eye contact. As I approached the last row, I noticed he was wearing Levi's and had a paper bag in his hand. I could see his hands and did not see a weapon, so I approached him slowly. I told him I was with the FBI and asked where the money was. He did not hesitate, never said a word, and handed me the paper bag. I then told him to stand up, and as he did, I grabbed his arm and walked him over to a wall, where I searched him for a weapon. He was very meek and complied with all my demands. I had probable cause to suspect him as being the bank robber, so I handcuffed him and opened the paper bag. Inside was paper currency, some bundled with straps with the name of the bank that had been robbed.

I asked the guy his name, and he gave it to me. I then escorted him out of the bus station and contacted the FBI office by radio, saying that I had the bank robber in custody and the money recovered. I asked one of the SAs at the bank to bring over the list that enumerated the serials numbers and year of the bait money. This bait list would verify if the money in possession had come from the victim bank.

Shortly after that, several SAs from the bank robbery squad arrived and brought with them the bait list. We compared five fifty-dollar bills in the paper bag with the information on the bait list, and they were identical. These SAs took custody of the bank robber and transported him to the office for an interview and processing. Case solved, money recovered, and subject in custody.

This person was later charged with the bank robbery, entered a guilty plea, and was sentenced to a prison term in a federal penitentiary.

———————

One morning we responded to a bank that had just been robbed not too far from our office. We arrived within minutes of the robber leaving the bank, but the vehicle he was seen leaving in was not located.

The investigation proceeded as usual, and the images on the surveillance video taken during the robbery were interesting. We had very distinct images of the robber and noted that as he was leaving the bank through the east doors, he was placing the money into the waistband of his trousers. A large puff could be observed emanating from where he put the money, and he started wildly dancing around outside the bank.

Occasionally a bank teller will provide a robber with a pack of money that contains a dye pack. After a short time, either a timing device in the pack or an electronic field located near a bank's exits will activate the gas to explode, emitting a red dye that tints the money, creating an enormous red cloud. (It is funny to see a car driving away with this red cloud streaming out the windows, drawing attention to the vehicle, and then the car stopping with the robbers leaving the vehicle.)

In this instance, the dye pack exploded just as he placed the money near his waist, but after dancing around, he kept running, jumped a wall, and entered his car. Fortunately, a witness coming to the bank saw this happen and obtained a partial license-plate number of the departing vehicle.

We continued the investigation, found the car, and talked to a young lady who looked at the photo of the bank robber. She said she recognized the young man as a friend who had used her car during the time of the robbery. She was furious with him for doing this and told us that he had left town almost immediately and told her he would get in contact with her at a later date.

Several days later, she called the case agent, said that this friend of hers was returning to Phoenix, and provided us with the flight information. It was an evening flight, so we had plenty of time to gather and devise an arrest plan. The SA had already filed a bank-robbery complaint against this thief and obtained a federal warrant for his arrest.

That evening, several of us proceeded to Sky Harbor International Airport to await this robber's arrival into Phoenix. We worked with airport security to assist us, found the gate he would be coming through, and waited for the arrival of the aircraft.

Shortly after that, the plane arrived, and passengers started passing through the gate, looking for friends and loved ones. We had to be careful because we wanted to make our arrest away from all the citizens, who did not know what was going on. We knew the robber would not be armed since he was on this flight, but we had to be careful nonetheless.

Within moments, the thief came from the ramp and into the terminal. We recognized him immediately, and we nodded to each other that this was the person we wanted. We allowed him to walk a short distance to get away from the throng of individuals exiting this plane. We then gradually approached him, grabbed his arms, and forcibly moved him to the nearest wall, identifying ourselves as we did so.

Needless to say, this generated quite an interest from all the people in the area, but airport security immediately calmed them down, and that allowed us to continue with the matter at hand.

We moved him to a small room to talk with him about the bank robbery, and we advised him of his Miranda rights after telling him that he was under arrest for the bank robbery. We searched him and noticed a large red mark on his abdomen. We asked him what happened (as if we didn't already know), and he said he was making some spaghetti and as he stirred it, some grease splashed on him.

We just laughed at this ridiculous remark. We were quite sure that spaghetti cooked in oil would not taste too good. He looked stunned when we would not believe what he said and more so when we showed him the photo of him leaving the bank with the appearance of dye gas coming from his waist area, the same area where he had the large red mark.

After a short time, he realized the futility of his nonsensical alibi and admitted to the robbery, providing us with specific details. He later entered a guilty plea to this crime and was sentenced to a lengthy jail term.

———

We were in our separate cars, just leaving the office to conduct routine investigations on cases we all were assigned, when the radio dispatcher voiced in with an alert that a bank robbery had just occurred in Marana, Arizona, a small community just northwest of Tucson. I was working with Reuben Martinez, an excellent investigative special agent, and we advised dispatch that we would be en route to Marana to assist the Tucson agents. Typically, the Tucson resident agency handled its own investigations. They had a veteran group of SAs down there, but they asked for some assistance because of the extreme violence that had occurred during this robbery and resulted in the wounding of one employee and the death of the bank manager. We drove code three down to Tucson and learned of the details of the robbery over the radio as we traveled.

Apparently, several men had entered the bank before its opening by confronting an employee outside of the building and, using her, forcing their way in. Once inside, they demanded the money, but since the vault was not opened because of the early hour, the manager tried to open it manually but obviously was quite excited and nervous. The robbers became irritated, and one of the men took a letter opener from a desk and stabbed the manager, resulting in his immediate death. They took what money they could find and stabbed the other employee, severely wounding her. They left and drove away in their car, which had been parked directly in front of the bank.

Prior to their exiting the bank, another employee arrived at work and noticed a strange car parked in front. She became suspicious, because the bank was not yet opened and therefore jotted the license-plate number down on a scratch pad. She then drove to a nearby store to call the police and report what she saw. When the police arrived, the car was gone, and upon entering the bank, they saw the devastation that had occurred. They summoned an ambulance for the wounded employee and immediately had her transported to a hospital, where she would later recover from her injuries. She could not be interviewed about the events of the robbery because of her severe injuries. She was immediately tended to by doctors and placed in the intensive-care ward. As a result, a good description of the robbers was not immediately forthcoming. She did mention to investigators before being transported to the hospital that both men who robbed the bank were very young and did not look like typical robbers, if there was ever such a thing.

A murder/bank robbery investigation was initiated, and every lead imaginable was checked out. Obviously, the first thing to be checked out was the license-plate number written down by the employee. A registration check determined that the license plate was registered to a car in Yuma. The SA who worked the Yuma territory was contacted, and he determined that this vehicle was currently at the house where it was registered. Due to the distance from Marana to Yuma, it was impossible for the car to be driven back home in that short period.

As a result, it was surmised that the employee had transposed the letters, the numbers, or both from this license plate. The employee was confident that the plates were from Arizona and not from another state. SA Colin Dunnigan was running the investigation for the FBI in Marana, so he started doling out leads, and when Reuben and I arrived at the bank, we went inside to find out what Colin wanted us to do. It was sad to see the manager still lying dead on the floor. He was just a hardworking bank employee who unsuccessfully tried to help the robbers get what they wanted. He did not deserve to die. In essence, we were now working a bank robbery and assisting local authorities in working the murder aspect of this case.

SA Dunnigan had been transposing the numbers and letters of the license plates in various combinations and handed us one of the combinations to check out. Once we ran a license-plate check, it came back to a vehicle that was similar in description to the car described by the employee who had seen the license plate and jotted the number down. Reuben and I went to the address where the vehicle was registered and, once there, spoke to an elderly gentleman who wanted to know why we were interested in the car. I explained to him that we were investigating a very dangerous bank robbery in which the vehicle could have been used. He said that was impossible since the car belonged to his daughter. However, she had recently been hanging out with several young men that he did not approve of, but he doubted that they would rob a bank. He then provided us with the address where they were living in Tucson. This address was in the northern part of the city, and upon arriving there, we noted that it was an apartment complex.

We deliberately and slowly scouted the parking lot of this complex and, from a distance, spotted a car similar to the description given by the employee who viewed the original license plate. This car had the license-plate information given to us by SA Dunnigan. We decided it would not be prudent to tip our hand by driving up to the car to examine it, so Reuben left our car and walked toward the suspect car, passing by it slowly and then returning to our car. He just looked at me and said something to the effect of "I think we have it. There is what appears to be blood on the door handle and the driver's window."

We contacted SA Dunnigan by radio, gave him our findings, and asked for more backup. Other agents started showing up to our location, which was several blocks away from the apartment complex. We did not want to cause a stir if anyone happened to be looking out the windows of their apartment and saw some cars with antennas on them in the parking lot.

We told everyone who arrived what we had found and what we suspected. I told them we did not want to confront anyone at the apartment parking lot in the event the presumed robbers were in the house and might see us. If someone else came out to the car and drove off, we would stop the vehicle several blocks away from the complex and see what we could determine at that point. We still did not have a real good description of the robbers other than they might be two young white males, one short and one tall.

After about twenty minutes, two young males came out of the apartment and got into the car with a young girl. We let them drive away, and when they were about three blocks away, we decided to stop the vehicle to find out who they were and continue our investigation. We had a marked police unit pull up behind them and light them up while tapping the siren of his patrol car.

The suspect car pulled over to the side of the road, and as they did so, several FBI cars pulled around them and blocked them from the front. The car that Reuben and I were in drove behind the suspects' car, and when they stopped, we both jumped out and ordered the occupants to get out of their vehicle. The young girl was driving, so we concentrated on the two young men. Reuben said he would take the guy who was getting out of the front seat, and I said I would take the guy who was stepping out of the backseat.

Once they got out, the taller and older of the two, who exited from the front seat, started screaming and demanding to know what was going on. The younger and shorter of the two males exited from the rear seat, and I grabbed him and forced him to the ground, yelling, "FBI." This younger guy shouted, "I didn't stab him; he did!" or words to that effect. The older one, who turned out to be his stepbrother, wanted to know what was going on, and so Reuben told him we were investigating a bank robbery. He just said, "Fuck you," and told his younger brother to shut his mouth. The older one then said that this was bullshit and demanded to be released. Both of them were handcuffed and taken to a police station for further questioning. The young girl was detained and interviewed, and the car was impounded.

Subsequently, it was determined that both of these young men were from Germany and living in the United States. The charges, including murder, would be filed by local authorities as they could receive capital punishment if convicted in state court, and that would not happen in federal court. Further investigation determined that the blood on the car matched that of one of the employees of the bank. Apparently, one of the robbers had blood on him from all the violence in the bank, and when he entered his car, he got it on the exterior.

Combined with all the other evidence collected at the crime scene and with other interviews, both brothers were convicted of the murder of the bank employee, sentenced to death, and were subsequently executed by the State of Arizona for this horrible crime.

A lot of work by the FBI, Marana authorities, and the Arizona Department of Public Safety went into this case and resulted in solving it. SA Dunnigan poured out his heart and soul to address this matter, and his dedication and assertiveness are what led to the ultimate resolution of the senseless, horrific, and unnecessary death of the bank manager and severe wounding of the bank employee.

———————

Late one morning, a call came from dispatch on all our radios that a bank had been robbed near the vicinity of Nineteenth Avenue and Bethany

Home Road. Several robbers had entered the bank, pepper sprayed some elderly people, and escaped with a large sum of money. Many FBI and police units responded to this robbery, and it was subsequently determined that there were several robbers, the number ranging from three to six, depending on the separate claim of each witness interviewed. Also, an audit determined that the robbers had taken more than $200,000. The Phoenix Fire Department and Rescue Squad also responded, treating and transporting to hospitals those who were injured during the robbery. SAs and Phoenix police detectives and officers responded, and within a very short time, a marked unit from the Phoenix PD located a car matching that used in making the escape. The getaway car was found about three blocks from the bank behind a large shopping center.

A subsequent search and examination of this vehicle yielded some latent fingerprints (prints that are found by processing the vehicle with a dusting powder or other method) as well as a loaded revolver. Further investigation determined that this car had been stolen earlier that morning. Although we scoured the entire area where the vehicle was located, looking for witnesses, we could find none who saw them transfer from this car to any other car or leave on foot through the shopping plaza. It was determined that this recovered gun had been stolen about a month before from a residence in Paradise Valley, a community just north of Phoenix and west of Scottsdale.

The investigation was conducted at the locations where the car and gun had been stolen, but these all met with negative results. However, contact was made with a detective from the Paradise Valley Police Department who had worked the theft of the gun the prior month, and he advised that he had no suspects in that case as the gun had been taken in a random burglary of a house when no one was at home. The detective informed us that he would start researching the many burglaries that occurred in Paradise Valley for the past six months and would go back further if necessary. After doing this, he provided us with a list of people possibly involved in some of these burglaries, none of whom had been arrested but were considered suspects.

Several of these suspects had fingerprints on file, so we gave the list to the Phoenix PD identification division, and—bingo—we got a hit on one of the prints found on the stolen car. They belonged to a juvenile, and things started coming together as witnesses all claimed that the robbers were youthful in appearance.

One interview was curious in that a bank employee said that one of the robbers directed the employees to a back room and used a specific term as to what this place was referred to. The name of the room was unusual, so it appeared that perhaps the robber had worked at a bank and knew how to refer to that room by name. We knew that this could be critical in solving this case.

Subsequently, the number of Phoenix PD robbery detectives and FBI agents determined that a long-term surveillance of the juvenile whose fingerprint was identified on the stolen car would ensue. The surveillance was initiated, and immediately many friends of this young man started associating with him as the party had begun. We could have arrested this juvenile on probable cause alone, but we wanted to capture as many of the gang as we could, so we decided to take our time and not rush into an arrest. This tactic resulted in the identifications of some other young males. However, we were not certain which ones were involved in the robbery and which were just hanging around to party with this friend, who now had a lot of money and was spending it on food, limousines, and other things to have fun.

Within two days, we were able to identify several of the suspects and found out that one of the friends was a college student at Arizona State University (ASU). This student had previously worked at this particular bank but had not entered the bank at the time of the robbery for obvious reasons; he would have been recognized. We found out that another of the suspects had a room on campus at ASU, so a search warrant was drawn up for this room. Some detectives and FBI agents went to this location at a time when some suspects were there, having a good time.

Upon arriving at the dormitory room, we identified ourselves, and the laughing and smirking of these suspects immediately changed to fear and anger. The search resulted in the recovery of just under $200,000.00 which was located in a cabinet in the room. When we were outside discussing which subjects were not in custody and what other work we needed to do, along came a shiny, one-year-old Corvette driven by the suspect who had previously worked in the bank. He did not know of our search or the arrest of his buddies as he drove up, showing off his new car. We commented how beautiful it looked as he parked, and he just smiled until I identified myself to him. I told him that he was under arrest for bank robbery, and he started denying anything about it. I placed him in the back of an FBI car, advised him of his rights, and began to interview him. He continued to deny everything, and I told him that we knew everything that had happened about this robbery and let him watch other suspects talking to other SAs and detectives in other cars. For all I knew, they could have spoken about the weather, and I let his young fellow know this. I also mentioned that they could be talking about their involvement in the robbery and implicating others. He shortly started crying and admitted that he had given these other robbers a floor plan of the bank but could not go in with them because he was known to the other employees. Also, he had a class that morning that he needed to go to. To demonstrate how naïve this fellow was, he asked what was going to happen to his new car, and I told him we were going to seize and impound it. (It would later be sold and the proceeds returned to the bank.) He did not think that he should lose the car since he paid cash for it, but I told him the loss of this car was the least of his problems.

This investigation eventually concluded with the arrest of all the subjects and the recovery of a substantial portion of the stolen money. All the subjects entered guilty pleas to bank robbery, and each received a prison sentence based on past criminal history. The juvenile whose fingerprint was identified on the car was remanded to state custody rather than federal custody because of his age. The irony of this is that the majority of these subjects were in their early twenties, but the juvenile was the ringleader of this whole group and led them down this path and right behind bars.

After everything had been said and done, I had a chance to speak with some of the parents, who were all devastated by what their sons had done. In fact, I received a letter from the student at ASU who had formerly worked at the bank, apologizing for his actions and asking me to try to use my influence to get him a reduced sentence. I could not do this for him, and it was unfortunate that these young men did not think of the consequences of their actions before they chose the path they did.

I have often thought of them and always hoped that they returned to society as fine young men, but to this day, I have no idea what courses they took in life after serving their prison terms.

Another robbery in downtown Phoenix was done by a black man who entered the bank, demanded the money, and left. We conducted the investigation without any definite clues but gathered what information and evidence we could. This case was assigned to me—the luck of the draw: no real evidence and no initial suspect.

A week later, the day before Thanksgiving of that year, another bank was robbed by a black male, but in this case, a license number of the escape vehicle was given by a witness. Subsequent investigation determined that this vehicle had been sold a week earlier at a used car dealership. Investigation at that dealership determined the date and time that the transaction was made: about two hours after the bank robbery in downtown Phoenix that had occurred in the past week. The salesperson also said he sold the car to a young black male and provided the best description he could, and that description was similar to that of the suspect in the robbery before Thanksgiving as well as the recent one.

Fortunately, the salesman had the name James Williams as the purchaser of the car as well as an address for Williams, and he also gave us full details of the car he had sold.

Several of us proceeded to the address, where we spotted the car. We observed several black males standing around outside, and one of them matched the description of that day's robber. We approached these men, and I called out the name that the car salesperson had given us. One man answered that he was Williams, and his demeanor was very pleasant and quiet. I told him I needed to talk to him for a few moments, and he came over to my FBI vehicle to speak with me and another SA. Several other agents spoke with neighbors and others in the area.

I told Williams that I needed to speak to him about a bank robbery that had occurred earlier in the day, and he said he would talk to me. After advising him of his Miranda rights, I just asked him if he robbed the bank, and he said he did. Wow, that was quick. I never expected him to admit that he robbed the bank. I told him that I was going to arrest him for the robbery, and he said that was fine, so I arrested him at that moment and placed him in handcuffs.

I told Williams that I was stunned that someone as nice as he was would rob a bank, and he said he needed money. At that very moment, one of the other SAs who was interviewing neighbors called me over, and I went to see what he wanted. He said that all these neighbors had told them that Williams had arrived at this location about an hour before with a backseat filled with frozen turkeys, which he distributed to all his friends who had very little money and were now going to have very nice Thanksgivings.

Apparently, right after the recent robbery, he had gone somewhere and purchased dozens of turkeys to give to the less fortunate. He was just trying to help others who had less than many other people, and he felt sorry for them.

I went back to Williams and asked him about this, and he said that is what he had done with some of the money and that he was going to go back out and take whatever money he had left to buy more food for these people.

Sure enough, after I had searched him and removed money from him, he said all that money was from the bank, and he asked if I could give it to one of his friends to buy more food since he was going to jail. I told him I could not do that as this was the bank's money and had to be returned. But he protested quietly and said it was his money since he took it from the bank. He then said he understood why I had to return it to the bank and just smiled but was a bit unhappy—not for himself but because he could not help out any more of the less fortunate.

Technically, we'd always seize everything bought with stolen money, but there was no way in hell that we were going to go to all those people and take the turkeys back from them to give to the bank. We later returned the money to the bank and told the security officer that we had not seized the seasonal birds. He had a laugh and said he did not think that the bank would insist on that recovery, and he was happy that these people had turkeys for Thanksgiving.

We took Williams to our office to fingerprint, photograph, and interview him before taking him to a federal magistrate for an initial appearance. During the interview, he provided all the information about the bank that he robbed, the turkeys he purchased, and the store where he purchased them.

I then told him that we'd had a bank robbery a week earlier, and it was my belief that he had also robbed that bank and used the proceeds to purchase the car he had. He vehemently denied robbing that bank but admitted to buying the vehicle with money that he had saved.

I told him just to consider the following: A bank in downtown Phoenix was robbed a week before. Two hours after that robbery, a car was purchased several miles away from that bank. Another bank in downtown Phoenix was robbed today. The robber escaped in the car bought last week. We found the car and determined that he was the person who purchased it and robbed the bank today. Was this just a coincidence, or was he responsible for both robberies? He just shook his head and denied robbing the other bank.

I then asked him if he knew where the bank that was robbed last week was located in downtown Phoenix, naming the streets that the bank was adjacent to. He said he knew where that bank was located. I asked if he had ever been in that bank, and he said no. I again asked him if at any time in his life he had ever been inside that bank, and he said he had not.

I then asked him if he had ever been in a bank where they had posts with ropes to guide the patrons toward the teller line and if he had ever seen them. He said he knew what I was talking about. I then asked him what he would say if I told him that his fingerprints might be on one of those metal posts in the bank robbed last week. Williams said that could not be the case because he did not go near the posts, did not touch those posts, and that his fingerprints could not be on them. I just looked at him, smiled, and told him to think about what he had just said. He cracked a smile and said, "Oh, shit. You got me."

At that point, he asked if I was mad at him for lying to me, and I said I wasn't and understood why he denied it, but now I wanted him to tell me all about it. He admitted to robbing that bank. After that robbery, he walked down to the car dealership that was located several miles away and purchased the car. He provided all details about both robberies, and, I have to admit, this was one of the easier interviews and admissions I ever had. I talked with the AUSA, and we charged him with two counts of bank robbery, and he later entered a guilty plea. He had no prior arrests, so the judge saw fit to sentence him to a jail term that was not extremely extensive.

Several years later, I received a telephone call from a federal parole officer who told me that Williams was getting out of prison on parole, and he wanted me to know that he would soon be back on the streets.

Several months later, a bank was robbed in downtown Phoenix, and after the description had come across on the police radio in my car, I got on the radio and advised the dispatcher that this was possibly James Williams, who was just released from jail. The dispatcher informed us that a Phoenix police unit had a car stopped with several black males in it and provided the location of this vehicle. I proceeded there.

Upon arrival at that location, I spoke with the officer who had stopped the car, and he said that this vehicle matched a description of one leaving the bank robbery. I walked over to the car, and, sure enough, Williams was standing there in handcuffs. As I approached him, he remembered me, calling me by my first name. I just said, "Why?" and he shook his shoulders and smiled.

Several detectives arrived, and since the majority of the work was conducted by the Phoenix Police Department, it was decided that Williams would be charged with the bank robbery on the state level rather than a federal level. Williams was accused of bank robbery, entered a guilty plea, and was sent to the Arizona State Penitentiary (ASP) in Florence. I never did see him again.

This incident involved a bank robber who had to be one of the nicest, friendliest, and most thoughtful criminals I ever came across. Williams just could not grasp the fact that what he was doing was wrong, but he never fought the fact that he had to go to jail and pay the price for his transgressions. Considering that the majority of bank robbers are cruel, cold, and calculating, he did not fit this mold, and it was sad that this man did things that put him on the wrong side of the law. Too bad, but if you commit the crime, you must do the time.

———◆———

On another occasion, I had a bank-robbery case assigned to me and had a vague description of the robber who escaped. We had a variance in the descriptions of what the robber looked like as he wore a hat pulled down to cover the upper part of his face.

The best description in this case was the car the robber used to get away from the bank. Although no license plate was observed, the car was described as several years old, either dark blue or black, and with a passenger door and hood that were different colors from the rest of the car. The right fender was severely damaged. The immediate thought was that this vehicle had been involved in an accident, and the passenger door and hood were replacement parts from a junkyard, and the right fender had not yet been replaced.

I worked this case for several days and was at the PXPD talking with several detectives also on this case. We decided to put out an audio BOLO to all police units and to alert the investigators if they located the car matching this description. The police unit was not to contact the person driving the vehicle but just get a license plate for further investigation.

As I was driving away from the police department and making my return to the FBI office, I was stopped in northbound traffic on Central Avenue, and the image of this car came to mind. I was stopped and looked to my left, saw the car next to me, and said to myself, *That's what the car would probably look like*. I kept looking at the car and the person driving it, and the driver resembled the bank robber from the scant description I had. I was stunned. This could be the car and the thief.

Traffic started moving, and I did not want to alert the driver of that car by stopping and getting behind it as I still needed to do a great deal of investigation to solve the case. So I proceeded with the traffic and drove a bit slower, hoping he would pass me up so I could get the license plate. However, I was not so lucky. He made a left-hand turn, so I got on the police radio and asked for any police units in the downtown area to be alert for the vehicle for which the BOLO had just been transmitted on all police radios.

I drove into the left lane and made an immediate turn westbound and then southbound when I arrived at the next block. Fortunately, I was able to get into position when I spotted the car again and see the license plate. I advised the police dispatcher to discontinue on my request for assistance from police units as I had already spotted the vehicle. I then returned to the PXPD and contacted the investigating detective again, and we worked on getting the registered owner of that vehicle. We also canceled the BOLO for the car.

It turned out that the person who owned this vehicle had recently been released from prison for earlier armed robberies as well as various drug charges. We were able to obtain a very current photo, so we made a photographic lineup to show to witnesses. Once we showed them this lineup, we obtained positive identifications that this was the bank robber. Based on these identifications, positive fingerprint comparisons of latent prints left at the bank, and the car description, I was able to establish sufficient probable cause to draw up a federal complaint and obtain an arrest warrant. We then set out toward this guy's address in order to arrest him for the bank robbery.

The detective and I arrived at the residence with several other detectives and knocked on the door. A young female tending to several toddlers answered, and we asked for the robber by name. She said he was not at home but should be back in about an hour. She was his girlfriend, and he was living at this residence with her. I explained to her what we were there for and asked if we could search the home. She allowed us to do this, and we opened up a dresser drawer in her room, and there was a pile of money. We went through it, and there was some bait money that we knew came from the bank, so we seized the cash.

This lady became irate and said that was her money from a welfare check she had received. I told her this money came from the bank, and she said that her boyfriend mixed his money with hers, but some of that money was hers. I asked her when she cashed her check and how much she received. She told me she had just cashed the welfare check yesterday and used a small amount to feed her children.

I counted the money, and the total did not coincide with the amount that was taken from the bank. So either she was lying, or her boyfriend took out a large sum, and that was why the amounts did not add up. I contacted the AUSA, who authorized the prosecution of the robber to discuss this dilemma. The AUSA asked me my opinion, and I told her I did not want to take it all because the woman had children to feed. I was comfortable taking the remainder after leaving her with what she claimed she had gotten from her welfare check with a little deducted for what she mentioned she spent on food. Personally, I felt sorry for her, but this money was not mine, and I could not just allow her to keep all of it. That was our ultimate decision.

Shortly thereafter, her boyfriend came home, and we arrested him for the bank robbery. He denied robbing the bank until I told him he had bait money in his possession, and then he just stopped talking. I also informed him that we had every right to confiscate all the money we located and explained our dilemma because of his girlfriend's claim to the money from her welfare check.

Now he had a problem. He could deny owning any of the money and put the blame on her, or just say that some of it was his and some belonged to her. He opted to admit to the robbery and tell us how much he took out. The amount he claimed to have spent combined with what we were confiscating nearly totaled the amount taken during the robbery. He said the remainder was her money from her welfare check.

She was crying as we removed him from the residence to transport him to jail. She was left to care for those children by herself as she knew he was going to be gone for a very, very long time.

One of the detectives came over and asked me if I wanted to donate some money to this lady for her children. I gave him some money from my pocket, as did all the other detectives and uniformed officers who were present. The robber thanked all of us as he watched us do this. I was not happy with him because he was abandoning her again, but there was nothing more that I could do.

We later returned the recovered money to the bank, and that included the cash recovered from the drawer at this residence as well as the money the robber had on his person at the time of his arrest.

The robber later entered a guilty plea and, considering his past criminal history, was sentenced to a rather lengthy prison term.

———◆———

I was sitting at my desk, working on a deadline report that needed to be sent to FBI HQ by the end of the day. It was late morning when a bank-robbery alarm came in, and a verbal page was put out throughout the office that a bank in Tempe had been robbed and all available SAs should respond. The supervisor came over to me and told me to remain in the office and complete the report as it was needed at headquarters. I did not have much more to do on it, but it still needed to be typed and proofread before going out.

I completed the report and took it to the chief steno to have it typed immediately, so we could send it out ASAP. This was done in no time, and after the report was completed, I went to the supervisor and asked if he knew how the investigation was going in Tempe. He checked and said they had quite a few witnesses and still needed some help, even though the robbery had happened about two hours earlier. I said I would go.

I went to my Bucar and got the description of the robber from our dispatcher. He was described as a young white male, about thirty years old, medium size, and his car as a white Ford Mustang with a partial Texas license plate. This car was possibly being driven by a young white female.

I proceeded to the bank and was about two miles away, driving east on the main surface street. As I approached an intersecting street, I observed a white Ford Mustang. This car was facing north, waiting for traffic to clear, so it could proceed westbound on the same street that I was on. As I passed, I noticed a female driving, and the passenger was a white male of about thirty years of age. I wondered if this was just a coincidence or if this was the same car used in the bank robbery. I am not a great believer in coincidences, so I considered that this had a real possibility of being the car, the bank robber, and his accomplice.

I went to the next block and turned around to get behind this Mustang that was now westbound. As I approached it, I noticed it had a Texas license plate with the partial plate information that was described earlier by our dispatcher. I notified the office of what I had and furnished them with the remainder of the license plate. I continued following the Mustang and kept the office and nearby FBI vehicles appraised of where I was and what direction we were heading.

The Mustang turned north on another main street, and I followed. Traffic was getting heavy, which was good as it gave me logical cover, but it also held up the other units that were trying to reach me and assist me in stopping this car. At one point, I inadvertently mentioned on the radio that we were going south, and, correctly, the FBI cars coming to assist me turned around. I then realized what I said, so I corrected myself, and the cars again had to turn around to change direction, further delaying them because of my verbal error.

The car then turned into a residential area, and I had to advance closer so that I would not lose sight of them. I notified everyone where I was by radio and then advised that the people in the car probably realized I was following them. The passenger kept turning around to look at me, and the female driver kept making turns as I continued to follow them. I needed to stay with them or risk having them escape.

After a few more turns, they turned into an apartment-complex parking lot, and I broadcast the name of this complex and told the office to get hold of the Tempe police and tell them I needed immediate backup. I did not have radio communication with the Tempe PD, so I needed to go through our dispatch to get in touch with them.

Sure enough, after driving through the parking lot for a short distance, they continued to the far end and turned left into a parking spot. I notified the office of this and then said that I was blocking the car in and would be confronting the subjects. I would be temporarily out of radio contact and asked dispatch to speed my backup. I still did not have any backup at this time, but I knew it would not be far behind as I could hear sirens in the distance getting closer.

Although I was alone and completely disregarding our rules for having assistance in making apprehensions, I needed to confront this couple as I was fearful they would leave the car and run into the apartment complex, and I would lose sight of them. I could not allow that to happen.

I pulled my car directly behind theirs to block it in and jumped out, drew my weapon, and identified myself as FBI. The male passenger got out, and I yelled at him to get down on the ground, and he started to comply. I also told the female who was driving the car to keep her hands up on the dash and in full view of the other officers who were there. There was no one else assisting me, but they did not know that. I was sure they believed that we had several units surrounding them. The female went into hysterics and started crying loudly. I told her to keep quiet, and as long as she didn't move, she wouldn't be hurt.

The male got down on his knees and kept watching me as if he was uncertain whether to run or not. He looked around to see who else was there, and I kept yelling at him to lie down on the ground and get on his stomach, and so he eventually complied. He just kept pleading with me not to shoot him.

At this time, I saw a Tempe police car at the end of the driveway and motioned him to come toward me. He saw me and approached quickly. He got out of his car, and I told him I had two subjects, one in the car and the other on the ground. He said he would take the female out of the car, and as he did, I went to the subject on the ground and handcuffed him. Now both subjects were in custody.

The female told the officer the address where they were both living. Other SAs and police detectives began arriving. The Tempe detectives said they could quickly get a search warrant for the residence where this couple lived, and I said to go ahead and do it as they had been working this case since its inception, and I just happened to arrive there. It was not clear at this point who was assuming jurisdiction and what agency would be prosecuting the case as federal and local prosecution were both satisfactory. The important thing was that we found the robber and had him under arrest.

The detectives worked very hard, secured the search warrant, and, upon searching the residence, found the money from the bank. We relinquished all custody and prosecutorial jurisdiction to local authorities, and the robber was prosecuted and convicted by the city prosecutor. The female was also prosecuted as an accessory to bank robbery.

It was amazing that I was able to go to the bank robbery two hours after it occurred, arrive at the same intersection at the same time the robbers did, and that we were able to effect the arrest without any incident. Talk about being in the right place at the right time—at least for me, that is. It was not too good for the robber and his female accomplice.

On one particular weekend, my wife and I took our boys camping in northern Arizona, and I took a vacation day on Monday to make it a three-day weekend.

On Tuesday morning, I walked into the office and checked my incoming box, where everything that was coming to me would be located.

I noticed that several new cases had been assigned to me, one of them a bank robbery that had happened the previous day. Usually, the case would have been assigned to one of the responding SAs who went to the bank and worked the case. However, on that Monday, we had several bank robberies that had been assigned to the other SAs, and since I was next in rotation for assignment, this one was given to me. It was no problem as this occasionally happened.

I checked with a few of the agents who went to this robbery to get the facts and find out what work had been done. All investigation would subsequently reach me by way of an FD-302, an investigative report that contained details of the investigation or interview results of a witness. But this might have taken several days or so to get to me, and I wanted to get a jump on this case, so I asked around.

Apparently, a bank located on the outer wing of a shopping mall had a drive-up cubicle separated from the shopping mall, approximately one hundred feet from the bank entrance. Every day, the female bank employee who worked in this small cubicle would put the money and records on a small cart and transport them to this cubicle.

On this Monday, she was wheeling the money out, when she was approached by a man she did not see. He demanded that she give him the money and not turn around, or she would be shot. She complied and handed him the bag containing money and did not look at him as he made his escape. I then learned that there was no additional existing evidence and no other witnesses to this robbery. I did not even have a description of this robber other than that he was a male and sounded young and Caucasian. There was no additional description.

Now some of these robberies are hard enough to solve when evidence exists, but I had virtually nothing. No wonder no other SA wanted to take this case, and I couldn't say I blamed them. So I just sucked it up and accepted the fact that the case was mine but vowed never to take another Monday as a vacation day.

I contacted the Phoenix PD robbery detail and talked to the detective who was working this robbery. He got on the phone and congratulated me for joining him in getting a case with no evidence. We laughed about it but said we would give it our best shot and take it as a real challenge to get it solved.

The detective said that he had a confidential source who lived in the neighborhood where the bank was located, and he would have his source try to find out what the word on the street was as to who might have committed this robbery. Good start anyway, considering we had no other real way to go in the investigation.

Several days later, the detective called me and said that his source had given him the names of a potential suspect and others who might have been involved. The talk on the streets was that a young white male named Jimmy Schwartz was the person who had taken the money from the drive-in teller while two other friends waited for him in a car about a block away. The driver was a young white man named Phil, and the passenger was a young white man named Bob Martin. He did not have a last name for the driver of the car. They associated with each other, and Jimmy did not live too far from the bank.

I obtained photos of all these young men and put together three separate photo lineups to show to the victim/teller in the event she saw them before this robbery occurred. Each lineup had the picture of each suspect along with five other photos of young men of similar appearance. I did not show her the separate photos of each suspect so as not to influence her decision on any identification.

Of course, as I expected, I had no luck of any sort with any identification. One thing I did find out, however, was that the person identified as Jimmy Schwartz had a checking account at this same bank at the shopping mall, but this was not unusual since he lived nearby. I had the bank provide me with all of his records about deposits and withdrawals but found nothing unusual other than that he carried a very small balance in his checking account.

The detective had his source try to gather any additional information, but nothing further was ever obtained. Little money had been taken from the bank during this robbery, so no large purchases were made by any of these three subjects.

Several months went by, and I spent my daily efforts working on cases with more promise of resolution and prosecution. However, this one was dogging me, even though no one had been hurt and not much money taken. I finally decided that I was going to make the first move.

I contacted Jimmy Schwartz by telephone and asked him to come down to the FBI office to talk to me. He asked what it was about, and I told him that I would discuss it with him when he arrived. I could hear the nervousness in his voice, but that was not unusual as many people would be a bit upset if the FBI wanted to talk to them. Nevertheless, he agreed to come down to the office, and so we set up a time for the following day.

The next day, he came to the office. I took him into an interview room and told him that I wanted to talk to him about a bank robbery that occurred in which his name came up. I even advised him of his Miranda rights.

I directly asked him if he was involved in the robbery, and he said he was not. He asked me how his name came up, and I just stated that I was investigating this case and that in talking with witnesses, his name came to my attention, and I was not going to elaborate any more. He was very nervous but again said he did not do the robbery. I tried to downplay it by telling him that this was the only time I was going to talk with him about it, so if he wanted to tell me, this was the time to do it. I told him no one was hurt and very little money was taken, so he should consider discussing it as it would be to his advantage. He didn't buy it.

I also told him that if he had done it and did not want to say anything more, he should just say that the interview was over. I did not want him to lie to me and subject himself to any additional charges of giving false information to a federal agent. This statement really got him going, and he became a bit agitated, saying he did not rob the bank and was upset because I did not believe him.

In fact, he told me he had often thought about becoming an FBI agent because that was his ambition in life. I said that was good as he had no previous record with the law. But he should consider the fact that having no previous arrest record would help him if he decided to confess to the robbery. He really became upset now. I could see that this was going nowhere as he was not going to tell me about this robbery. I told him that as long as he was going to insist that he did not do the robbery, this interview was over. I further told him that I knew he committed the robbery and that the next time I saw him, I would be putting handcuffs on him. I then escorted him to the exit and told him to leave.

I returned to my desk and wondered what to do next. I knew the cat was out of the bag now and was positive he would be telling his buddies about this interview and my attempt to have him confess to the robbery.

I told the detective working this case with me about the results of the interview. He had been unable to take part in the interview because of a prior commitment, so we met for coffee and talked about what we would do next. We decided to wait a bit to see if his source could find out anything more. We waited for several more months, and nothing was forthcoming in the investigation. I was beginning to believe that until we got more information, we might not ever solve this case.

Then one day the detective called and told me that the passenger believed to be in that car the day of the robbery, Bob Martin, had just been arrested on some minor drug charge and was currently sitting in a cell at the Maricopa County jail. We thought this might be an excellent opportunity to conduct an interview and see if we could get any more information.

The detective and I went to the jail and had Martin removed from his cell and put in an interview room. We identified ourselves to him and told him we were going to interview him about a bank robbery that had occurred. The first thing we did was advise him of his Miranda rights and cautioned him not to say anything that was false because if he did, I would consider charging him with providing false statements to a federal officer. At this time, I removed a small card I had made up showing Title 18, Section 1001, of the US Code, which defines this charge. I earlier made a copy of it, laminated it, and tossed it at him. He read it and said that he understood and that he would not lie to me.

I told him not to say anything at that time. The detective and I had earlier agreed that we would throw out some facts to Martin to show him that we knew quite a bit about this robbery. Then we would see how he reacted and would continue the interview from that point.

I told him that I knew that he, Phil, and another friend named Jimmy Schwartz were involved in the robbery of the bank, naming the bank, the address, and the date the robbery happened. I also told him that he was just a minor player in this robbery and that the purpose of this interview was to get it resolved since not much money had been taken and no one had been hurt. Also, it was Jimmy who had confronted the teller, and Martin had just sat in the car with Phil. He had a minor part in the robbery, and if he thought it might be to his benefit to help us, we would see if the minor drug charges he was facing and for which he was now in jail could be lessened. If we were not successful in having them reduced, at a minimum, we agreed to talk with the prosecutor to advise that he was cooperative in our investigation. I then told him that now was the time to speak if he wanted to. His eyes widened, and he said, "Wow. You guys know everything that happened. What do you need me for?"

Finally, we could hopefully get to the bottom of this and get it over with. I told him that even though we knew what happened, we needed him to tell us in his words. He said that there was no sense in lying because of all we knew, so he agreed to talk.

He told us how Jimmy approached the teller, took the money from her, and returned to the car and then jumped in and told Phil to drive away. When he said this, I told him to slow down as I was writing it all down, and when I got to the name Phil, I stopped writing, shook my head, and said, "What was Phil's last name again?" as if I already knew it. He said, "Andrews."

I said, "That's right. Phil Andrews," and told him to continue. He finished telling us about what happened and that they were disappointed they had gotten such little money to split three ways. It had not been worth the risk of robbing a bank to get such a small amount.

We thanked him and said that we would be getting back with him at a later date. When we left, the detective said he would contact the prosecutor who had charged Martin and advise him of his cooperation. I said that I would do a background check on Phil Andrews to see what I could find.

I determined that Andrews still lived at home with his parents and found out where he worked. I decided that Andrews should be interviewed as soon as possible before he learned that we had obtained his name from Martin.

The next day, I drove out to the site where Andrews worked, approached the foreman, and asked to speak with Andrews. His foreman asked if there was a problem, and I said that I just needed to ask him a question or two and would be through with him in a very short time. He called Andrews forward and put us into a room so that I could talk with him.

I told Andrews who I was and that I was investigating the bank robbery and asked him if he wanted to talk to me. His face went white, and he had a hard time talking before he started to say anything. He said he did not know what I wanted from him and was not willing to talk to me. I told him that was fine, but I knew he was involved in this bank robbery as an accomplice and gave him my name and telephone number in case he changed his mind. He and I left the room, and he returned to work.

I went back to my car and drove off. I went around the block, stopped with a view of the business parking lot, and waited. After about ten minutes, I watched as Andrews came out to the parking lot, got into a car, and drove away. I followed at a safe distance, calling for several other cars to assist me in this moving surveillance. There was one other FBI car in the vicinity, so he helped me keep an eye on the car that Andrews was driving.

After a short time, Andrews drove up to a residence and entered. It turned out to be the house where Jimmy Schwartz lived. It looked like I had struck a nerve, and we were on the mark.

I then drove to where Andrews lived with his parents and knocked on the door. His mother answered, and I asked her if I could talk to her. I told her what was happening and that I had tried to talk to her son, but he refused to speak with me. She obviously was very upset, and I tried to calm her by telling her that her son had very little involvement in this robbery. I then said that it was just a stupid mistake, but it would be better if he provided a statement to clear it up and explain what he had done.

She said she did not know what to do and asked me if I could return when her husband was home. I said I would, asked her to tell her husband to call me, and told her I would answer any questions they might have. I felt very sorry putting her through all this, but she would find out sooner or later that her son was involved. I wanted her to know that we would be as fair as we could with her son. I felt that if she knew me from speaking with me, she might be a bit more comfortable with me, knowing that I had been honest with her.

Later that afternoon, her husband called to ask me what was happening and if I could come back to the house. I explained what had occurred and that I had tried to talk to his son, who told me he did not want to talk to me. The husband said, "He does now." He asked me to come back to the house and said that he would see to it that his son would talk to me and get this straightened out. I said I would be right over.

When I arrived, I met the father and greeted the mother and their son, Phil. I then went over all the events and said that I knew about his involvement in the robbery and wanted his side of the story if he wanted to talk about it. I also said that he should only talk to me of his own volition and not because his parents might be forcing him to. I then suggested that he could have an attorney guide him if he so desired.

Phil said that he wanted to tell me about what happened as he had always felt bad about being involved with the other two associates, whom he had met only a short time before the robbery occurred. Phil was a very decent young man who made a stupid mistake and was too afraid to take a stand against the other two. He was afraid that if he said anything about them, they would perhaps harm him or his family. I told him that would not happen and took a statement from him, providing me with all the details of the robbery as he knew them, including the fact that he had received some of the stolen money.

I presented this matter to the AUSA, who authorized a complaint charging Jimmy Schwartz and Bob Martin with federal bank robbery. Phil Andrews was not charged and agreed to testify against the other two if this case went to trial. The matter was presented to a federal grand jury to get Andrews's statement on the record, a true bill was voted, and an indictment followed for Schwartz and Martin. Federal warrants were issued for their arrests.

The following morning, I went to locate and arrest Jimmy Schwartz and learned that he was not around as he had enlisted in the military, possibly the navy, and was leaving that morning to the recruitment center to be processed out.

The detective and I rushed over to the recruitment center and checked with military personnel, who said they were expecting him to arrive at any moment as he was going to be shipped out. I told them there was a slight problem and that he was going with us and not with the navy that day. This upset them greatly as they were on quota and now would have one fewer to report.

Within ten minutes, I could see Schwartz running up to the doors of the recruitment center. Just before he entered, I approached him outside and asked if he remembered me. He looked at me and said that I looked familiar, so I took out my handcuffs, showed him, and asked again. He was stunned as I told him he was under arrest for the bank robbery. He said he could not go with me as he had just joined the navy and was getting ready to leave. Obviously, he was in a state of shock. The cuffs went on.

We walked him out to our car, and he started crying, telling me I had just screwed up his life. He calmed down after about twenty minutes and asked me what was going to happen. I explained the procedure to him and said that he was going to answer to the bank-robbery charges. He still insisted that he had not committed any bank robbery. He said that if I could just let him join the navy, he would leave and never return to Phoenix. I told him that I did not have that discretion and that if he had talked to me about the robbery the first time I met him, I might have been able to work something out with the AUSA and any attorney who represented him. We then took him to the federal building to begin the process.

As I tried to find out where Bob Martin might be so he could be arrested, I determined that he had already enlisted in the military, and I found out where he was stationed. I contacted our agents in the nearest city to where he was stationed, where they located him and placed him under arrest.

Both Martin and Schwartz entered guilty pleas to the bank-robbery charges. The ironic thing was the sentencing. Schwartz, who was not in the military, worked with his attorney to convince the judge to place him on probation and allow him to join the military. The judge accepted this agreement after determining that the military would receive him with the conditional phrase that if he were discharged before his commitment date, he would be returned to this judge for resentencing. In other words, any early release such as dishonorable discharge, AWOL, or anything else could result in his being returned to the court for any future possible jail term.

Martin, who was already in the military, was discharged following his arrest and guilty plea and was sentenced to a jail term, not a lengthy one but a jail term nevertheless.

Phil Andrews was not charged with any crime due to his cooperation and lesser involvement in the case.

The best part, on a personal note, was being able to approach my colleagues on the bank-robbery squad and show them that the detective and I had been able to get a break in this case, solve it, and obtain convictions and sentences.

———————◆———————

The supervisor of the bank-robbery squad received a telephone call from a southeastern FBI office. We learned that two men involved in a series of bank robberies in that part of the country who had outstanding warrants for their arrests could be located in the Phoenix area. They had been involved in shootouts with authorities and were considered armed and extremely dangerous. That office provided our supervisor with the specific information they had developed and requested that we locate and arrest these two men.

The supervisor assigned this case to an SA who called a short meeting of our squad and set forth the details he had been given as well as what he had determined since receiving this information. His investigation concluded that these two men had arrived in the Phoenix area by airline several days earlier, but he had no specific information regarding where they could be at the time. He provided all of us with photos and descriptions of these two men and told us to be on standby. Once he determined additional information as to any specific location, he would contact all of us, and we could proceed to locate them and make the arrests.

Nothing further developed that day, so we all went home for the evening. At about midnight, we each received a telephone call from the office and were told to go to a particular location in Scottsdale, a suburb of Phoenix. Upon arrival, the case SA grouped us together and told us that both men were staying at a small casita at a luxury resort in Scottsdale. These small casitas were separate rooming houses located on the grounds of this resort, and those men had arrived several days before and had been staying in a designated casita.

We all went to the resort, and several SAs went to the resort office to talk with the night manager. It was about 3:00 a.m. when we all learned that the case agent had verified the specific casita they were renting and that they were checking out first thing in the morning for a late-morning flight out of Arizona. We had plenty of time, so we devised a game plan on how we would make the arrest.

We knew that we would not sneak up and bust in on them as it was too risky with many other vacationers renting adjoining casitas, and there was always the possibly we would be noticed since the casita was on open grounds. There were just too many casitas near the targeted one, and we did not want to cause any situation that might generate gunplay with these two men. The risk was just too high, knowing the propensity for violence of these bank robbers. We finally decided on an arrest plan that would isolate the two men, separate them, and immediately place them under arrest, negating any violent action on their part.

Since they had told the resort desk they would be leaving in the morning, they had done the check-out procedure the previous evening. We knew we had to keep watch on the casita, so they could not sneak out during the night even though we had no reason to believe they would leave. We placed a few SAs in a position where they could watch the targeted casita and alert us if there was any movement from within.

Early the next morning, one of our SAs called the men to thank them for their stay at the resort and told them we had a courtesy ride to the airport for them unless they had a rental car to return. They did not list any vehicle information on their registration card, so we were not certain if they had a rental car. The subjects were elated and said they did not have a rental car and appreciated the offer from the resort. They said they would be ready to leave shortly and gave us a time. We said that we would have a courtesy car quickly brought up for them at their casita.

We knew this was our best opportunity to make the arrest since they were going to the airport and would not have any weapons on them. These weapons would be packed in their luggage, if they had any at all.

After a very short time, I drove the courtesy car to the front of the casita, parking on the street approximately 150 feet away from the front door. We had about eight SAs total working to make this arrest, so the other SAs secreted themselves near large shrubbery so that they could not be seen from the casita. These SAs acted as if they were other residents or employees of the resort and would not look out of place if they were seen wandering around the grounds.

I walked up to the door of the casita, knocked, and announced that the courtesy car was there to take them to the airport. One of the men opened the door with a huge smile on his face, and there was no question in my mind that this was one of the men we had photographs of. He greeted me and thanked me for coming to take them to the airport. I asked him where his luggage was, and he pointed to four large suitcases and a carry-on bag. I told him I could take all the bags out to the car, but it might take some time as the car was parked a short distance from the room. I suggested that if they did not mind and would help me carry the bags out, it would be easier, and we could leave sooner. They had absolutely no problem with this. I jokingly said I would take the smaller bag, so both of them picked up the two larger bags and started walking out of the room toward the car. Perfect. Their hands were now occupied carrying luggage, and this would lessen any violent action on their part when confronted by the arresting agents.

About midway to the car, I could see SAs starting to approach them from their cover, so I went up to the subject directly in front of me, grabbed on to him, and said, "FBI." He was startled, and at this time both of them were taken down to the ground by all the SAs who were there. They were handcuffed, and the case agent came up and told them that they were under arrest for bank robbery. They strenuously objected, but once we showed them their photographs, they stopped yelling and asked for an attorney, saying they were going to sue us.

One SA took all their luggage and put it into an FBI car to take to the US marshals office. The US marshal would subsequently be taking custody of both men to transfer them back east to stand trial for their crimes. One of the subjects was placed in the backseat of an FBI vehicle for transport to the FBI office, and the other one was placed in the backseat of the FBI car assigned to me, with another SA sitting in the backseat with him. After a brief moment, I got into the driver's seat of my Bucar to transport this subject to the FBI office for fingerprinting and photographing. The fugitive looked at me, surprised, and asked me if I was the courtesy driver for the resort. I said that I was. He then asked if I also drove for the FBI. I told him that I drove for a number of companies including the FBI, and he commented what a great job that must be.

Nothing further was said, but I think he later realized that I was not just another courtesy driver but an SA who had assisted in a scam to bring them out of their room to the waiting arms of the FBI.

———————

It was July 1, 1982, and I was going to take several hours of vacation time on this day. I was taking my wife and the four boys to northern Arizona to a small lake for a weekend of camping and fishing. It was extremely hot in Phoenix, and the weekend break was something we all were looking forward to. Several friends of ours had already left and arrived at the campground. We were going to meet them, and they were going to reserve a campsite near theirs, so we could all have a great time on this holiday weekend.

I called Rosie and told her I had a bit more work to do before I left the office to come home and leave on the trip. She said the camper was packed and ready to go, and the boys were all biting at the bit, waiting for me to come home so we could leave.

Shortly after I hung up, a bank-robbery alarm sounded, and the bank robbery was announced by the dispatcher to all mobile units and all SAs in the office. I was just getting ready to leave when this alert sounded, and I waited for a minute or so to hear what was going on. The robbed bank was in South Phoenix, so I told the supervisor I would head down there. He said we probably had enough SAs to handle the robbery, and by the time I got there, there would probably be nothing to do. I said I would finish cleaning my desk off and putting everything away. I would then decide if they needed more help, and if they did, I would go to help them.

Just then I heard that there had been gunshots fired somewhere near the bank and an officer was down, and that immediately made my decision for me. I told the supervisor to call my wife and tell her that I was working a bank robbery, and she and the boys were just going to have to wait until I returned home.

I jumped in my car and headed straight for the bank. I learned through a PD radio communication that there were shots fired at a nearby neighborhood bar and an officer was down. I found out from SAs at the bank that they had enough SAs at that location to interview witnesses and continue the investigation, so I said I would be heading to the bar where the shots were fired.

Shortly thereafter, I arrived at this lounge that was surrounded by ambulances, police cars, and the media. I identified myself to one of the police officers who formed a perimeter around this bar, and he allowed me entry. As my eyes adjusted to the darkness after coming in from the bright sunlight, I noticed two people being worked on by paramedics in the middle of the room. A short distance away, paramedics were working on another person lying on the ground. These paramedics were extremely efficient in handling this chaotic scene, considering all the people who were there. I saw a few robbery detectives whom I knew and went over to see what I and other SAs could do to assist if needed. They said they could use a few SAs to help interview witnesses, so I got on my portable radio and requested assistance from some of our SAs, who responded immediately and came to the bar to conduct interviews.

It was then that I leaned over to view the two detectives who were lying down by each other and recognized one of them as a robbery detective I knew very well and who was highly respected. His name was John Davis, age forty-eight, well respected in the African American community and all of Phoenix. He was a huge man, both in size and character. He was well known for mentoring young men who were taking the wrong path in life and were on the road to jail. He was not the type of person to coddle these young men but to sit them down and, in his soft, determined voice, make sure they knew where John was coming from. There was no question that when John talked to them, he commanded their respect and saved many of them from going down that wrong path.

The other officer who was down was a detective I did not know, and his name was Ignacio Conchos, age forty. He did not work on the robbery detail at the PXPD but was assisting John Davis in helping work the robbery on this day.

The other person being worked on by paramedics was later identified as Efren Contreras Lopez, an illegal alien from Mexico. He had fictitious identification on his person, but we later identified him through finger-prints as Efren Lopez.

Shortly after the robbery had occurred, SAs and detectives were interviewing witnesses at the bank, so John Davis and Ignacio Conchos had been detailed to conduct a neighborhood investigation by contacting businesses in the adjacent area in efforts to identify and possibly locate the bank robber. They decided to go to the bar to see if anyone there had seen a person matching the description of the bank robber. When they entered the bar, they approached the bartender, identified themselves, and asked him if he had seen a person matching the description they provided. The bartender told them that a man matching that description had come into the bar just a short time earlier. He pointed to a corner booth located at the rear. As John and Ignacio turned to look where the bartender was pointing, the person in this booth, later identified as Efren Lopez, raised a semiautomatic handgun and started firing at the two detectives. He hit both of them, and they fell to the floor. Ignacio Conchos was fatally wounded, and as John Davis fell, he drew his weapon and shot back at Lopez, striking him, and he fell to the ground. John then had the presence of mind to radio in that shots had been fired in this bar, and two officers were down. PXPD radio immediately dispatched a code 999. Whenever this code was sent out, police officers from all over responded because that meant that one of their colleagues needed immediate assistance and was probably severely injured, if not worse.

Other officers were there within moments since many were already in the area working the bank robbery. Paramedics were also there immediately and started working on all the individuals who had been shot. It can best be described as controlled chaos, and the best of care was being provided to all who had been shot.

Once everything was brought under control at this location and there was nothing left to do, I returned to the victim bank. I was a bit shaken after seeing a good friend shot and lying on the ground, not knowing if he was going to make it through the night. I had a hard time working but knew things had to be done to wrap this up as the bank robber needed to face justice for this robbery and shooting.

Arriving at the bank, I saw that much of the investigation was completed, and those in command were starting to release everybody to return to other work. It was getting into the early-evening hours by the time I went back to the office. I did not feel like going on the camping trip, but there was nothing I could do at the office, and so I told the supervisor I was leaving to take my boys camping since I had promised them, and they were still waiting for me. He knew where I would be camping as it is our procedure to have an itinerary posted as to the date and times I would be at any one location. He said he would contact me if needed but to get away and try to enjoy the time with my family.

I finally arrived at home and loaded up the family for the three-hour trip up north. Arriving there, I found our friends, who had been wondering where we were. I told them about all the events of the day as the one friend was an SA I worked with who also knew John but did not know what had happened. I briefed him on all the circumstances and told him that when I left, John had been alive and his condition upgraded but that Ignacio Conchos had died.

The following day, we went to a nearby small town to call the office and find out how John was doing. The last word was that he was fine and in stable condition. We returned to the campsite and told our wives of John's condition. We stayed the weekend through July 4 and then returned home. I went back to work on July 5.

We went to see John in the hospital, and the first week was very rough on him. He was in a lot of pain, and he was groggy from all the medication they were giving him. We kept in close touch with him to keep his spirits up, and he seemed to keep getting better as time went on. We all prayed for him and were hopeful that this great man would pull through all of this.

Our office contacted FBI HQ and advised the appropriate personnel there about these shootings. There are procedural issues that need to get done for insurance purposes and so on when a local police officer is shot and killed in the line of duty. One thing our office did was recommend that the FBI director send a signed citation to honor John Davis for his quick thinking in stopping the felon before he could harm or kill anyone else. His extremely brave actions were extraordinary, considering that John was severely wounded as he halted the criminal from shooting other people. If he had not done this, there was no telling how many more people would have been shot and killed by this panicked murderer.

Several weeks after this incident, the citation signed by FBI Director William Webster arrived in the Phoenix office. Several of us SAs who worked with John went to the hospital and presented him with it. When we arrived, John was sitting on the edge of his bed, talking with his beautiful wife, who was with him at all times. We presented this citation to him, and he had a great big smile on his face. He then said he was getting stronger and stronger every day and was hoping to be going home in a week or so. What great news this was for all of us.

On August 7, 1982, I got up early to get ready to go to work and went into the bathroom to shower and shave. I turned on the radio, and when the news came on, the announcer stated that Detective John Davis had passed away on the evening of August 6, 1982. I was just stunned, and my hands were shaking. I looked at myself in the mirror as tears welled up in my eyes (and still do as I write this). How could this happen to such a grand person, highly respected by all? I woke my wife up to tell her just before I left for the office. I will always remember that day as all of us at the office were shaken by this traumatic turn of events.

Apparently, infection had set in while John was in the hospital. John was a hefty man and had received a gunshot wound to the stomach area. While the doctors were able to work with him to save him early on, he remained in the hospital because they were worried about this infection that eventually took his life.

A number of us SAs attended his funeral in a packed church. John was loved by the entire community, and this was evident by the number of people there. The services for Ignacio Concho were separate and also heavily attended by police officers and the entire community.

Efren Lopez recovered from his wounds inflicted by Detective Davis. He was subsequently convicted of two counts of murder and was sentenced to life incarceration at the Arizona State Penitentiary in Florence, Arizona.

Please take a moment of silence for John and Ignacio for their sacrifices.

CHAPTER 2

Fugitives

———◆———

SOME OF THE MORE INTERESTING facets of criminal work are the location, identification, and apprehension of subjects who are wanted by police agencies for crimes and are on the lam. Fugitive work is interesting because fugitives will do anything to keep from being located and arrested, and law-enforcement officers will try to outwit the fugitives and their methods in efforts to apprehend them. Numerous methods are used to get information on the fugitive's location, including complete background checks, ruses, and interviews with friends, enemies, family members, and anyone else who may have knowledge of where the fugitive may be. Once located, then it is necessary to try to apprehend the fugitive without violence if at all possible. Many times, once the fugitives realize that they are about to be arrested, they resort to violence in an effort to escape. Some will meekly surrender once they realize the inevitable, but many will not.

The most successful SAs who worked fugitive cases were those who were resourceful, imaginative, and dedicated. Obviously, we operate within the law in how we proceed to locate the fugitive. Being very imaginative is essential as it is a cat-and-mouse game with the fugitive trying to outsmart the hunter and the hunter trying to outguess what the fugitive will be doing to escape. The hunter draws on his or her skills and imagination and uses methods, ruses, or anything else that will snare the hunted. Each and every fugitive case is unique and has its specific drawbacks and possibilities for success. Considerable deliberate planning and organization are mandatory to arrest the fugitive in the safest manner possible.

Hanging on my wall is a plaque bearing the following statement: "There is no hunting like the hunting of man, and those who have hunted armed men long enough and liked it, never care for anything else thereafter.—Ernest Hemmingway." This statement says it all, and any fugitive hunter will attest to it.

Phoenix Division Desert Hawk fugitive task force insignia

Author with FBI Director Louis J. Freeh

Desert Hawk fugitive task force members with Director Freeh

MCSO Lieutenant Pat Cooper - MCSO Sheriff Joe Arpaio - Author

A fugitive task force code-named Desert Hawk was established in 1992 in the Phoenix division. A local internal FBI study determined that at that time, there were over thirty thousand outstanding arrest warrants in Maricopa County, Arizona, many of them for very dangerous felons. A fugitive task force was considered, and once approval was obtained from FBI HQ in Washington, DC, contact was made with the Maricopa County attorney's office to run our plan by them. A county prosecutor was advised that the FBI was planning to put together a joint task force that would be operated with FBI funding, and this prosecutor agreed with this premise in efforts to reduce a large number of existing felony warrants.

Elite officers from a number of local, state, and federal agencies would be asked to be part of this task force. Those selected would be tested for a period of time to see if they could fit in the mix with all the officers assigned to the task force. They would have to agree to work all hours of the day and night as needed and forfeit other plans if there was a need for them to participate in locating violent fugitives. They would be given additional extensive proper training to work as a group and be required to attend firearms-training sessions weekly and attend a course at the FBI Academy in Quantico, Virginia. The work would be extremely dangerous, so it was very important that this task force work as a unit to ensure complete safety for all participants. After a trial period, all their actions would be assessed by me and Lieutenant Patrick Cooper from the Maricopa County Sheriff's Office, who helped supervise this group of highly trained and efficient men and women. Desert Hawk was a sub squad operated under an FBI squad overseen by SA Supervisor Steve Chenoweth.

Those selected officers who were doing well stayed on, and those who did not fit were asked to return to their respective agencies. Some decisions were difficult to make but had to be done because all lives depended on having the best candidates working with each other. The task force would be a work in progress, and all means would be taken to ensure accuracy, control, and safety in our work. Desert Hawk was provided with sufficient funding from the FBI, and monthly financial accountability was essential to ensure we never ran out of funds when they were needed most.

The county attorney agreed that this could actually help alleviate the huge backload of warrants and offered full support in backing this proposal. As a result, various police agencies in the Phoenix metropolitan area were contacted in efforts to obtain personnel who could assist on this task force. As mentioned, Lt. Patrick Cooper, an extremely experienced, competent, and efficient officer from the Maricopa County

Sheriff's Office, came to help lead this task force. In the formulation of this task force, we decided that all personnel coming to us from all these agencies had to be handpicked with their own department supervisors' recommendations. This task force was going to be very demanding and dangerous. The targeted fugitives whom we would seek to arrest had to be considered extremely dangerous and/or extremely hard to find, so it was essential to have the best officers available to find these elusive and dangerous felons.

As a result, after many interviews with different officers and agents, a total of fifteen sworn officers were assigned to the task force, and all agreed to the terms that were set out. The local officers were sworn in as federal agents so they could effect federal arrests, and the federal agents were sworn in by Maricopa County Sheriff Joe Arpaio so they could make arrests on the local warrants. Many states consider federal agents as peace officers who can effect an arrest at any time. Arizona does not, so all federal agents had to be sworn in by the sheriff to make it all legal.

Once Desert Hawk began operations, all funding came from the federal government, and some local officers brought in vehicles that could be used for undercover work. Old trucks, panel trucks, beat-up cars, and anything that could not be considered "police-looking" vehicles were used with great effect. These officers were given leeway as to dress code for the day, and many of them dressed down so as not to appear to be police officers. It was a relaxed atmosphere in an intense environment. Without a doubt, Pat and I could not have selected a better group to do this taxing work. It wasn't that we never had any disagreements. That was to be expected in this type of environment with very aggressive, brave, and dedicated officers who had no qualms about voicing their personal opinions on any issue that might arise. But once the disagreements were sorted out, we all pulled together for the success of the missions. We knew that it just was a matter of time before we would have extreme violence in our fugitive apprehensions, and any one of us could be killed on any given day. Therefore, we engaged in a tremendous amount of training in arrest and firearms techniques. Every person assigned to this task force traveled to the FBI Academy in Quantico for extreme fugitive training that benefited all of us. In addition, we had a short qualifying firearms session weekly to maintain our firearms proficiency.

In fact, one time we went to an outdoor facility in the desert that had paintball guns, so we could practice apprehensions. It was in the form of a small western town, and we had control of the entire facility. We made several of our guys the bad guys and told them to do what they wanted and hide out, and the rest of us would work to locate and arrest them. We put our team together to find the enemy and set out. It worked out pretty well except for a few things that went wrong. We located one of the subjects and had him surrounded, so he could not get past us. I decided to move my position a bit to the right to get a better view, and as I stepped back, I backed right into a cactus (remember, this was in the desert just outside of Phoenix). The cactus went right into my back through my thick shirt. I was stuck and bleeding and in tremendous pain. But I could do nothing but jerk away, causing me to make a loud sound and letting the enemy team know where I was. In all this commotion, the subject started to run away, being shot at by others with their paint guns. I started running also, with cactus spikes in my bleeding back, and then I was shot in the back with a paintball. So I was not only hurting from the cactus but also from the paintball striking me, and I was considered dead and out of commission for the remainder of this practice session. Who said this fugitive work was fun and exciting? I never found out who shot me, but we—let me rephrase that—*they* all had a good laugh when it was over as they helped pull cactus needles out of my back.

Once we developed the Desert Hawk task force, we found office space and assigned everybody desks, telephones, portable radios, and whatever else we needed. As time went on, more funding became available, and we were able to purchase sophisticated body armor in the form of jean jackets that could be zipped up the front and easily put on. We then bought extra handcuffs and leg irons for everyone. Although each officer brought his or her own weapon, we were able to provide several of them with shotguns. We had a magnetic sign that could be put on the side of one of the trucks that read A AND D PEST CONTROL, displaying a photo of a hawk with its talons around the neck of a rat—rather ingenious of the guy who thought it up. "A and D" actually stands for "armed and dangerous" in police jargon. We used this ruse on several occasions in order to get close to several fugitives, so we could apprehend them.

Our primary goal was to locate the more violent fugitives who were wanted by authorities and those who might have been missing for a substantial period. We had no problem with any one officer having only one case of importance and working that one case for a week or longer as occasionally this would be necessary to locate the person who was wanted. Once the subject was found, the troops gathered, an arrest plan was formulated by the officer whose case it was, and we set out to make the arrest. Superb operations were done by dedicated and brave agents who loved this type of work.

The following cases are related to fugitive work and how these arrests were made. Some were simple, and some were hard, but all were successful.

My undercover vehicle on fugitive task force

Fugitive task force practice schedule

Firearms practice with fugitive task force

Jumping walls

Salvaged bumper from FBI vehicle after ramming
vehicle of fleeing fugitive

In one instance, we had been looking for a fugitive to arrest and learned through our background investigation that he loved cars. Once we located him and started following him in our cars, he pulled into a strip mall and got out of his vehicle. I drove up next to him driving a stylish shiny red Mitsubishi GT-3000, a real sporty and great-looking car. Naturally, as I drove up and parked next to him, he just looked over at me and started commenting about this car as I was getting out of it. I raised the hood and let him look at the engine so he would be distracted as the other officers made their approach. As he leaned over looking under the hood, four other officers approached him from behind and made the arrest. He never saw them because of his intense interest in cars.

———◆———

On another occasion, we had located a fugitive who was working at a small carnival that had set up in a suburb east of Phoenix. The case agent walked through the festival and saw the fugitive operating a shooting gallery where one could pay a fee, be given a small rifle, and shoot at stationary targets such as moving metal ducks and flying metal birds. If you hit enough targets, you received a little rubber duck as a prize. Win more, turn in the rubber duck, and get a bigger prize. If you spent about thirty dollars and hit enough targets, you'd receive a larger prize that cost about six dollars—a real bang for the buck.

We did not know if this fugitive had any weapons with him, but because of his proximity to the general public, we did not want to find out the hard way, so we developed a pretty simple arrest plan. I approached him and pulled out some money to shoot at the targets. He was congenial enough as I said I wanted to win the big prize, so he handed me the rifle, which was attached to the wooden frame by a cable. I took several shots and started complaining loudly that this gun was shooting high, and it would take a miracle to hit anything. Now the last thing he wanted was someone complaining and chasing off other customers. So he came over to me and looked at the rifle. He said the sights were fine and handed it back to me. I aimed the rifle toward the targets, took another shot, and then asked him to look down the barrel as I held it out. He again came over and looked at the rifle as I explained the problem. Once he was engaged with me and I had his complete attention, several other SAs and officers casually walked over and grabbed him, pulling him over the counter and to the ground. He was completely surprised and initially thought he was being robbed. Once we had him out from behind his barrier and searched him, we were assured he did not have any weapons and placed him under arrest. In addition, he did not have any weapons secreted on his side of the counter as we had initially feared.

We located the owner/operator of this small carnival and told him he needed someone else to work the shooting gallery. He was not very happy with us for taking away his employee. However, before we left the area, we looked back, and the gallery was operating again with someone else working it. I guess it was just too profitable to shut it down for any length of time.

———

One of the Desert Hawk team members had a confidential source who was going to advise him when a wanted fugitive returned to his apartment. For several days, we sat near this residence, waiting for him to come back but without any luck, so this source was recontacted and agreed to alert us when he returned. We went away and worked on some of our other cases.

In time, the case agent received word that the fugitive had returned to his apartment and that a few moments later, a female had gone into the apartment. We were working another case, so several of us broke and went to the area to assist the case agent in locating and arresting the fugitive. Once we got there, we still had to determine if he was in his apartment. The source said she did not keep an eye on the apartment the entire time since she had first notified us, so the possibility existed that he and this girl could have left without being seen. We decided to establish a ruse to see if he was in the apartment and then continue to make the arrest.

I went over to talk with the manager of the complex, identified myself, and asked him about the renter. I got little information from this manager as he did not know the person well other than that he was an occupant of that particular apartment. I told him we planned to arrest him and asked if I could borrow a company shirt that was used by employees. He went to a back room and found one that fit me. I then took a small water sprayer we kept in one of our cars and walked over to the apartment, appearing to be an employee coming over to spray for bugs.

I knocked on the door and got no response. I announced myself as an employee of the complex and said that I would like to gain entry to spray for bugs. Still no response. I turned the doorknob, and the door opened up. Surprisingly, it was unlocked, so I surmised that they must be there as the door probably would have been locked if they had left.

I entered the apartment as the remainder of the team stood to the side of the door and windows, so they could not be seen from inside the apartment. I loudly announced that I was an employee of the apartment complex and was going to spray for bugs, spraying a mist of water throughout the apartment as I whistled and appeared to be working. I then came to the bedroom door, knocked, and heard no response. So I opened the door, and as I started to go into the room, I noticed the girl and the fugitive lying in bed, and both appeared to be sleeping. The fugitive stirred a bit and looked up. I apologized and told him I was just spraying for bugs and would return later to finish up. He said that would be fine as she was still sleeping, and he did not want to wake her. I asked if I could finish spraying out in the living room area, and he said that would be OK.

I closed the door and continued spraying, making a bit of noise to override the small amount of noise being made by the remainder of the team entering the living room. The team had heard our discussion, and as they entered the apartment, I pointed out by nodding my head that this was the fugitive and that he was in the bedroom.

The team went in with force and immediately arrested the fugitive without incident. As the guy was leaving in handcuffs, he just shook his head at me like he did not know what was happening to him. He apparently still believed I was an employee of the apartment complex.

I later returned the shirt to the manager and thanked him for his assistance. He just smiled and said that after I left his office, he had watched the entire thing unfold as our team went in and arrested our fugitive.

———

Danny Snodgrass, a Phoenix police officer who was assigned to Desert Hawk, came over and asked me if I would go with him to arrest a female who had several outstanding drug warrants. Danny had made several contacts with her in the past and found her to be either easygoing or irate. It all depended on the circumstances at the time when he approached her. He expected that she would not be too happy with us since we would be arresting her.

She was kind of elusive and was not living where he had usually contacted her in the past. But he knew some of her friends, and coming into work that morning, he had spotted her car at a trailer park in north Phoenix.

Danny and I went to this location, and her car was still in front of the trailer. That did not mean she was there, but at least her car was. We decided to park a short distance from the car, and if she came out, she would have to come through the gate of a chain-link fence that surrounded this trailer. Once she was through the gate, we would approach her just before she entered her car. That way, if she saw us and tried to run, she would have to stop to open the gate, and that would give us the opportunity to close in on her and arrest her.

We sat there for about thirty minutes before we noticed her come out of the trailer and start walking toward her car. She opened the gate and closed it behind her; at that time, we got out of our car and walked toward her. As we approached, she looked up, recognized Danny, and asked him what he wanted. Danny told her he was holding several outstanding warrants on drug charges for her, and we needed to take her in. He was direct in what he wanted and was being very kind to her, hoping she would agree to go with us. Wrong.

As we grabbed her arms to handcuff her, she started pulling back and screaming for her boyfriend, who was in the trailer. Just then the door to the trailer opened, and her boyfriend started yelling at us. Her boyfriend knew Danny from past altercations and yelled at him, telling us to let her go or he would come over. One thing I learned about Danny: no one threatens him.

Danny looked at me and said he would handle the male subject and that I should handcuff her. He let go of her arm and started walking toward the gate to confront her boyfriend. He let him know that if he came out, we would arrest him for interference and impeding a legal arrest. As Danny did this, she lost it and started pulling away from me and swinging with all her might. She was like a wildcat trying to get away, swinging and scratching as she did so.

I had been in altercations with males on several occasions but never with a female. I had no reservations about hitting a man if I needed to try to subdue him. But I was hesitant about hitting a woman and was just trying to keep her in custody by wrapping her up and handcuffing her. She never once slowed down with all her wild antics, and I once thought of slamming her to the ground but was fearful of hurting her. So I just kept trying to hold on to her and handcuff her as she struggled and continued scratching me.

I looked up, and Danny was returning after telling her boyfriend to go back into the trailer or be arrested; the boyfriend complied as he did not want to go to jail. Danny grabbed on to her arm and told her to settle down, and she started kicking and continued her wild ways. Finally, we were able to put her on the ground and get the handcuffs on her but not before she scratched and kicked us several times. Once handcuffed, she started crying and settled down, and we were able to get her away from there and take her to book her into the county jail.

If I had a choice as to whom I would have to have a physical confrontation with, it definitely would be a male subject. Although a male may be stronger, at least we would be on equal grounds, and I would not hesitate to hit him. I just found that hard to do with a woman. In fact, Danny told me he heard all her screaming and yelling as she was pulling and scratching me. He had to smirk as he watched me trying to hold on to her without hurting her. But he also agreed that some of the hardest arrests he made were of violent females. Fortunately, not many of them had been willing to be punched by an officer, so many of them tried to stay calm without a physical altercation. That did not happen in this case.

Danny later told me she was very upset when he had her charged with resisting arrest and assault. Thank goodness she was in jail, and we did not need to arrest her on these additional charges. Hopefully, her attorney was the one who broke the news to her. I wonder if she scratched and kicked him.

———————

On one occasion, a female SA named Cathy approached me and asked if I could help her in locating and arresting a fugitive. The problem was that her initial investigation had determined that the fugitive was possibly living in a trailer approximately sixty miles west of Phoenix in the middle of the desert. She had driven out there to observe the trailer and said there was no way to approach without being seen. Again, it was in the middle of the desert between a few small hills. Any cars or anyone approaching could be heard or seen.

I told her we would go to the location the next morning, so the following day we got into my Bucar and proceeded there. After about an hour or so, we were driving on a dirt road and came around a small bend and over this little hill, when the trailer came into view. There was one vehicle parked in front, so we just casually drove up, stopped behind the parked car, and approached the trailer. I knocked on the door and said nothing. No one answered, and there was no noise in the trailer. I knocked again and announced ourselves as federal agents, but still no one answered. So I said out loud to Cathy, "Looks like no one's home. Let's leave and come back tomorrow."

She looked at me strangely, wondering why I would come all this distance only to return to Phoenix without having done anything further. I just put my hand out, nodded, and gave her the keys to the car. I then whispered to her to get into the car and drive away; I was going to stay there for a short time. She nodded, took the keys, and went to the driver's side of the car, entering and slamming her door closed. I opened the passenger's door as if to get in but stepped back, slammed the door, and went quietly to the rear of the trailer. Cathy started the car and drove away.

Things were silent as I watched her disappear over the small hill and out of sight. I stood at the end of this trailer, peering around the side and watching the door. After a minute or so, the door opened, and this young lady stuck her head out and started to come out. I stepped out and said, "Hello."

She yelled out, completely startled by this verbal invasion. She meekly returned my greeting as I got on my portable radio and told Cathy to come back as we had someone at the trailer. I asked the young lady if anyone else was there, and she said there wasn't. I cautioned her about lying to us since if there was someone else in the trailer, she could be charged with providing false information to a federal officer as well as being accused of harboring a fugitive. She said she was not lying and told me that she would allow us to search the trailer if we wanted. After Cathy returned, we did a careful search of the trailer but did not find anyone else there.

The lady said she did not answer the door earlier as she was afraid she might get in trouble, so she acted as if no one was home. She has not seen the fugitive for a short period and had no idea where he was. Cathy did an excellent job of conversing with this young lady and brought her into her confidence. We knew that this was going to be a hit-or-miss case, and all we wanted was for the fugitive just to turn himself in. If he would, we would not be out there again. If not, she could expect visits all the time. She said that if and when she saw him again, she would tell him. We left without locating our fugitive, not because of our efforts but simply because he was not there.

Cathy laughed all the way back to Phoenix about how we tricked the lady into coming outside. If I recall correctly, Cathy later told me the fugitive was arrested back east in another city shortly after this attempt, so perhaps the young lady was telling us the truth about his not being there for quite some time.

Another SA asked me for assistance in locating one of the fugitives he was hunting. He said that about twenty years earlier, a young lady named Linda Watson had been arrested in New York on a felony warrant; the arrest had occurred on the sixteenth floor of an apartment complex. Once Watson had been taken into custody, she had asked the arresting officers if she could use the restroom before she was taken to jail. One of the officers went into the bathroom to make sure there was nothing present that could be utilized as a weapon and looked out the window to the street sixteen floors below. Satisfied that they would not be compromised, they allowed her to go to the bathroom. After a few moments, it became very quiet in the bathroom, and one of the officers knocked on the door but received no response. The bathroom door was locked, so they rapped again and called her name, but again there was no response. They broke the door open, and Watson was nowhere to be found. She had apparently opened the window and crawled out onto a small ledge. She then crawled along this ledge to another apartment, which she entered from an open window and made her escape. An immediate search was initiated, but she could not be found. Watson was gone for the next twenty years.

The SA told me he had information that Watson was currently living in Phoenix under an assumed name and was a very respected and successful businessperson who worked in real estate. He was not positive that the person residing in Phoenix whom he had identified as Mary Williams was Linda Watson, his fugitive, but his investigation determined that it was possible. He could not ignore the chance that Williams could be Watson.

He obtained a current driver's license photo of Mary Williams and compared this picture to the photograph of Linda Watson, but that earlier photo had been taken when she was much younger. While there was some similarity, there was not enough to positively ID her. The SA had a set of fingerprints that were taken from Watson when she had been arrested many years earlier. So our task was to get the fingerprints of Mary Williams somehow and compare them with the fingerprints that he had of Watson. He did not want to go directly to Williams and ask to look at her prints because she had the right to refuse, and he did not want to alert her. So we sat down and developed a plan.

The SA had already conducted a discreet surveillance on Williams and knew the time she left home in the morning and the route she took to go to work. The following morning, we set up surveillance near her house, and as she left for work in her expensive car, I casually drove alongside her, passed her, and when I had the opportunity, pulled slowly in front of her as we approached a red light. We were both in the right-hand lane to turn right at the intersection. Another SA had his car immediately behind her. When everyone was stopped at the light, I slowly backed up close to her car, and the SA behind her pulled close to her rear bumper and slightly nudged her, causing her to put her car in park and get out to see if there was any damage. We all got out of our cars and identified ourselves as FBI agents. I told her that two days earlier, there had been a prisoner escape at the La Tuna Correctional Facility in Texas, and there was the possibility that she was the one who had escaped. We told her that we would have to take her to FBI headquarters to see if she was the escapee from La Tuna.

Williams was very upset as she knew that she was not the escapee we were looking for and said that she had to get to work. I then told her that we could resolve this rather easily if we could just compare her fingerprints to those we had for the escapee from La Tuna. She was happy to oblige. I looked at her fingers through a fingerprint glass and compared them to the prints of Linda Watson, the fugitive who had fled twenty years before. The fingerprint card was folded over so she could not see any information.

I determined with 100 percent certainty that the fingerprints were identical and that she was the fugitive we were seeking. I told the SA to hook her up and arrest her. She went ballistic and said she was not the fugitive as she had been in Phoenix for months and could prove it; she had never been to La Tuna. Then I told her that she was right—she was not the fugitive from La Tuna; she was the fugitive who had escaped from the officers in New York twenty years ago. She was absolutely stunned and was at a loss for words as she tried to process what was happening. She was still confused about the fugitive from the La Tuna prison. I told her that her fingerprints matched an old fingerprint card of hers from years ago and had nothing to do with any escape from La Tuna. She again went ballistic and said that she could not be arrested because we lied to her. When I explained that what I did was completely legal, she exclaimed that she was going to sue me and the FBI. (She never did sue us since she probably asked her attorney about it and was told that we were allowed to do what we did.)

We allowed her to make a telephone call so that a relative could come and retrieve her car (which was not damaged by the nudge). As she was being led away in handcuffs to be taken to jail, she looked at me with disdain and told me that as long as she lives, she will never trust the FBI again.

Well, I thought, I guess I won't sleep well tonight knowing another fugitive is mad at me.

———◆———

One very early morning, I was straightening out my desk before hitting the bricks to look for fugitives. Dave Schuminski from the Maricopa County Sheriff's Office came into the room with a member of our task force and announced that he had located one of the fugitives assigned to him. The fugitive was working at a local distribution company, and Dave needed some help from a few of us to pick this guy up. Danny Snodgrass and I, along with Greg Dykstra, SA Steve Fillerup, Greg Lauchner, SA Ron Myers, SA Keith Tolhurst, and SA Roger Browning, decided to help him out. The location where the fugitive worked was quite large, and Dave felt that it would be a good idea to have a number of us there to seal off the area in order to prevent this felon from running off. This group of officers and agents, with the exception of me, were the "heavies and runners" and could always be counted on to make any arrest.

Upon arriving at the business complex, Danny and I went into the main entrance and contacted an employee sitting at a desk. I displayed my credentials and asked for whoever was in charge. He asked if this was a joke, and I assured him it was not. He then said that he could help us, so I gave him the fugitive's name and photo. The employee stated that he did work there and, in fact, was right then working in the back warehouse. He continued to smirk, thinking this was a joke. Danny contacted Dave by radio and advised him what we found out about the fugitive and instructed him to come into the main entrance. We learned that the back warehouse was quite large, and if a group of us walked back there, the fugitive could possibly see us and run. As a result, we decided to have the employee page the fugitive by name and ask him to come to the front office, which was not an unusual thing to do.

The fugitive came up front within a few minutes, and as he came through the door, Dave and several others grabbed him and arrested him without incident. The employee behind the desk started laughing, still thinking this was a joke. He then realized that this was for real when he saw the handcuffs on the subject as he was being led out of the building.

I asked him what was so funny about all of this, and he requested to see my credentials again. I took them out and showed them to him, and as I did, I noticed that someone had taped a small symbol over my photo. It was the symbol of the Jack-in-the-Box hamburger chain: a little white round face with a pointed hat. As a result, the employee had thought we were playing a joke on the fugitive, and he was just going along with it. I just shook my head, removed the taped symbol, and showed him my actual photo.

We all had a good laugh over this, and I walked out thinking to myself that one of our guys pulled one over on me. I had a strong suspicion it was Danny Snodgrass. Danny and I started working together quite a bit when we formed the task force, and I developed a tremendous respect for this man. He had the drive and intuition one needed to have in locating and arresting violent fugitives. We became very good friends and remain so to this day.

Danny was the type of person who loved to have a bit of fun mixed in with the labor-intensive work we did, and he became my number-one suspect. I believe he grabbed my credentials earlier that morning as I was looking for something in my desk and taped the symbol over my photo.

No one ever admitted it, but there is no question that Danny had a hand in it.

———◆———

On another occasion, Dave Schuminski contacted several of us and said that he had located one of his fugitives working at a construction site on East Thomas Road. Again, the heavies and runners came along, and we met Dave at a designated location as his partner kept an eye on the subject, who he could observe working at this job site. Dave gave us the necessary information on his subject and showed us his photograph. His subject was a tall, muscular Hispanic male who was known to be violent and confrontational. We had sufficient manpower, so after we obtained the information from Dave, we went to our designated areas, surrounding this fugitive.

The officer who had been watching this guy all along advised that he had just gone into the outhouse on the job site. This made it a bit easier as we could now approach the area quicker and maybe get to him before he left the outhouse. Unfortunately, as we were approaching it, he came out and immediately spotted several officers walking toward him. He suddenly stopped, and as he did, Dave told him that we were with the police and to not make any quick moves. Dave called him by his name, and he immediately said he was not that person. We were all standing around him, and Dave asked him for identification. He started arguing with Dave as his eyes darted among all of us as if he was preparing to make a run for it. Danny Snodgrass grabbed him from behind, and the fight was on. This guy was strong and massive. He was very hard to get to the ground, and at one point, he reached into his shirt pocket, threw something on the ground, and started stepping on it. I recognized it as a small plastic bag containing a substance that looked like marijuana. Someone yelled at him as the fight continued, and he continued to try to step all over this plastic bag. I picked the bag up and retained what was left, which later tested to be marijuana.

After this brief struggle, we held him on the ground and handcuffed him. He was very belligerent, but after being told by Dave what he was being arrested for, he denied the charges. Dave then told him that he would also be accused of assault on the officers, possession of marijuana, and destruction of evidence. He finally settled down once he realized there was no sense in continuing to fight and argue, so we put him in the backseat of a car to wait for a marked Phoenix police unit to arrive and transport him to jail.

While he was sitting in the car, he pondered his dilemma and asked me what the charges were, so I gave him the list of charges that were the basis of the existing arrest warrant as well as an assault charge, the drug-possession charge, and the destruction-of-evidence charge. I then threw in that we might also charge him with cultivation of an illegal substance, just to get a response from him. He just looked up and asked what I meant by that. I told him that once he started to ground the marijuana into the field, there was the possibility that in a year, some seeds that were ground into the dirt might sprout into plants, and so he was cultivating marijuana. At this point, he started crying uncontrollably and asked us not to charge him with that—he had just been trying to get rid of it, so he would not be accused of a possession charge. I told him that if he behaved from there on in, we would consider not charging him with cultivation. At that point, he stopped crying, smiled, and actually became a very nice guy, telling us that he had been planning on turning himself in the next day (which we hear all the time). Shortly thereafter, he was transferred to a police car that had arrived to transport him to jail, and as he left, he smiled at all of us and apologized for all the fighting he had done.

Dave subsequently had him charged with assault and possession. He did not charge him with the cultivation of marijuana because, in reality, this was not something we wanted to accuse him of.

———————

A young first-office special agent named Dave told me that a fugitive case had been assigned to him and asked if I would be available to give him a hand working the case. I told I would and asked him for the necessary information.

Dave said an ex-con had recently been released from prison, where he had been serving time for murder. Apparently, this fugitive, whose first name was Alan, had decided to rob a liquor store in Kansas City, Missouri. After robbing an elderly lady who was an employee at the store, Alan hit her over the head with a large, blunt object, almost killing her. Alan escaped, and investigation by authorities determined he left the State of Missouri and was possibly headed to Arizona. As a result, the FBI in Kansas City obtained a warrant for unlawful flight to avoid prosecution (UFAP) and sent this information, as well as the description and photos of Alan, to the Phoenix division. This case was then assigned to Dave.

Dave said he had already obtained some background information on Alan and found out he might have a relative living in the Phoenix area, and Dave was in the process of determining this. He also learned that Alan had a small red car. Dave was going to do a bit of surveillance in an effort to gain additional information and would contact me once he found anything out.

A few days later, I had just completed working a bank robbery and was finishing up at the crime scene at the bank, when Dave contacted me by radio and asked if I was available to help him out. I told him I could and asked his location. Dave said he was on the west side of town in a community called Peoria and was in his car, watching a residence where a small red car, a Subaru, was parked. The streets in this area were complicated and not the typical cross streets found in most locales. Nevertheless, he directed me, and after seeing his car, I parked several spaces behind him and entered his vehicle. He was parked around a corner about half a block from the targeted residence, so he could not be seen by anyone looking out a window of the home. He showed me the photo of the subject as well as providing the physical description. Alan was a white male, about five feet, ten inches tall, 240 pounds, and extremely dangerous. Dave had already called the office for backup so that we would have additional SAs in the area in the event we needed them to help make the arrest if this happened to be the place where Alan was living.

After several SAs responded by radio that they were en route to assist, a very large man approached the Subaru and opened the trunk, placing something into it. After we looked at this person through a pair of binoculars, there was no question that he was the fugitive named Alan. Unknown to us at this time, he was reportedly leaving the area to go to San Diego to participate in some type of power-lifting competition. The trunk of his car stayed open as he placed several items in. At this time, he was joined in the yard by a young woman. It appeared to us that he was getting ready to leave, and the last thing we wanted to do was allow him to enter his car and drive away, necessitating a moving surveillance. This was dangerous as it could result in losing him or getting into a high-speed chase, endangering the general public. Dave asked the assisting SAs if they were nearby since we wanted to make the arrest before Alan got into his car. They responded that they were blocks away, but as was the case, the local roads went in circles and had dead ends, and our location was hard to find.

Dave started his car, turned right, and drove slowly toward the red car and the two people in the front yard. Alan was by the trunk of the car, arranging things, as Dave drove up behind. We slowly opened our doors and approached him, identifying ourselves as FBI agents and yelling, "Get on the ground!" or words to that effect. Alan glanced over his right shoulder toward me and immediately ran forward and jumped into the Subaru through the open passenger door. I yelled out that he might be going for a gun in the car and started running toward him with my weapon drawn.

As I approached the driver-side door, I could see both his hands with nothing in them. He had somehow been able to get into the driver's seat of this very small car, climbing over a gear shift that was on the floor. He was starting the engine and had one hand on the steering wheel. I heard Dave yelling at him to get out of the car as I jumped into the Subaru, kneeling on the passenger seat and yelling at him. I reached out and placed my hand on his neck as I kept my drawn weapon near my body, away from his grasp. His eyes were wide open, and he was reacting like a wild animal as he got the car started, placed the shift in gear, and drove forward with a sharp lurch. I lost my balance from this sudden action and, realizing I was in a moving car with this wild person, holstered my weapon and dove toward the steering wheel, forcing it to the left and trying to steer into the front of a car that was parked across the street. Just prior to hitting this car, Alan hit the brakes, stopping and again throwing me off balance while at the same time swinging his right arm, hitting me in the face, and driving me backward. I had been able to turn off the car by slamming the gearshift into park and turning the key. I tried to remove the key and throw it away but could not remove it from the ignition switch.

As he hit me, I swung back, hitting him in the side of the head, and this punch had virtually no effect whatsoever. He reached back and re-started the car, placed it in gear, and drove forward in another hard lurch. I jumped back toward the steering wheel and pushed hard left as he pushed hard right. I then let up and pulled the steering wheel to the right with him, and the car made a sharp right turn, running into the curb and stop-ping as he hit the brake. I turned the key again, reached over, and got him in a headlock, pulling him over my lap as I fell back into the passenger seat. I had a death grip on his huge neck, and he did not have any leverage to break loose from my hold. During this time, I saw in my peripheral vision that Dave reached over and removed the keys from the ignition, throwing them away from the car. Alan bit Dave severely on his arm as Dave tried to assist me in this fight, causing him to retreat backward out of the car.

Alan's head was on my lap as I held him, and I noticed his arms stretched toward the floorboard, moving very fast. I reached down to control his arm and felt the barrel of a gun in his hands. I reached for my gun and realized it was not in my holster. Apparently, during this wild struggle, my gun had dislodged from my holster and fell to the floor, and Alan now had possession of it. I yelled that Alan had the gun so that Dave would be aware of it.

I reached down again, felt the gun (a 2.5-inch .357-caliber Smith and Wesson), and realized that the barrel was pointing toward his chest. I was able to get my thumb near the trigger and thought of pulling it but then realized that if I did, the bullet would go through Alan and exit his body into mine as I was leaning over his back. Not smart at that time. However, I came to terms that I could die if I did nothing to stop him.

It's funny how fast all of this happens and how time slows down to almost slow motion or speeds up to a very rapid pace. Gunshots that are deafening on the gun range cannot even be heard or are small pops when one is engaged in these types of crisis events. These are all part of the body's defense mechanism for survival.

As I fought Alan for the gun, his two-handed grip on it was stronger than mine, and he pulled it out of my hand. I tightened my grip on his neck and instinctively reached for my shirt pocket, where I had an ink pen. I took it out and felt for his eye with my left hand, which was still holding on to his head and neck. I pushed the pen forward, intending to put it into his brain through the soft tissue in his eye. As I did this, he apparently knew what I was trying to do and lifted his head a bit, causing my pen to miss the eyeball and move along the left part of his face. I thought it had gone into his eye, and the next thing I knew, all hell broke loose.

I cannot recall exactly what occurred during the next minute as for some reason my brain has caused me to blank it out. However, from what I later learned from witness testimony, a violent fight occurred between him and me, with both of us exiting the car through the passenger door. The side-view mirror broke off, and one of my shoes came off. The next thing I realized, his arm was around my neck, and he was holding the gun to my temple as we struggled alongside the car. I was not going to be a hostage, and, believing I had already put out one eye, I extended my right thumb and swung it outward and toward his other eye. I missed my target, and my thumb went directly into his mouth. He bit down and ground on my thumb, trying to bite it off. I was able to extract it and break loose from his grip. Now I faced this wild man from a distance of about five feet with the gun pointed directly at me. I slowly backed away and waited for the flash of a gunshot as I was now convinced I was about to be shot by this fugitive, who was hyperventilating and shaking as he proceeded to walk toward me.

I know this is hard to believe, but it is the truth. It has nothing to do with bravery or anything else, but I just came to terms with the fact that I was going to die and came to accept that fact. I was not fearful of dying but was hoping that Rosie and the kids were going to be able to handle this fact. Now all I had to do was wait for the bullet to strike. I initially became very relaxed, but this did not last for long.

He turned around and backed up toward the car, sat on the passenger seat, and reached back, looking for the keys in the ignition so he could start the car. The keys were not there as Dave had earlier removed them. He lowered the gun to his side as he leaned back into the car, and I made a mad rush toward him, foolish as it seems. That was my gun, and I was furious that he had it and was going to use it to kill me. However, he heard me coming and raised the gun back toward me, causing me to retreat. With his wild eyes, he again started walking toward me, grunting and yelling, and again I thought I was going to die.

Just then I heard a gunshot and realized that Dave had been yelling at him, and when Alan looked to his right toward the voice, he returned fire back at Dave. I did not have any backup weapon with me, so I was completely unarmed. I dove to my right, getting behind the front of the car. I heard another gunshot and watched as Alan shot toward Dave and then lowered the gun in his hand. The gun then went off again, and Alan fell down. I thought Dave had shot him, and I started to move toward Alan, but then I realized that he had started sitting up. Alan had blood coming from his leg and could not stand; he was trying to get up but was having a hard time. Apparently, when Alan had lowered the gun, he pulled the trigger and shot himself in the leg, causing considerable damage to his lower extremity.

Just then an elderly lady came outside of the house near where the disabled car was parked; she wanted to know what was happening. I yelled at her to get back in the house, fearing that Alan would try to go over to the house and hold her hostage. I ran toward her, and she immediately retreated into the house, locking her door.

At this time, the other SAs arrived after maneuvering through all the streets, trying to find us. Also, a marked police car came down the road and pulled up near where Alan was sitting and bleeding. The officer got out of his car as Alan held on to the police car to try to stand and then aimed his gun at the officer. The officer got behind his vehicle and removed his weapon. He was unsure what was happening as he was just responding to a report of shots fired and had no idea who this person was. I yelled out who we were and that Alan was a federal fugitive who had already fired shots at us.

We now had Alan surrounded, and at this time, he started putting the gun to his head, threatening suicide. He continued doing this for a period of time until he weakened from blood loss, at which time SAs and the police were able to approach and arrest him. He was taken to a hospital for treatment and then transferred to jail.

I needed treatment for my thumb that was bleeding, and after later finding out that Alan had hepatitis B, I needed several shots to counter that.

After this incident was over, Dave and I were critiqued about the entire scenario, and all witness were interviewed. Both Dave and I were criticized as well as commended for our actions, and to this date, I have no qualms about what we did. We did not get into any high-speed chase but contained the incident to the local area. The only ones suffering injuries were Alan, Dave, and me, and I can accept my injuries. Apparently, it was not my time to die that day as I am still alive and kicking.

Alan was subsequently charged with assault of federal agents, and we went to trial. He was convicted because of the outstanding prosecution of the US attorney prosecutor, charging Alan for the separate violations on both Dave and me. Alan was sentenced on all charged counts and received over ten years' incarceration. After he was released, he would be transferred to Missouri, where he would be charged by authorities with the assault to commit murder for the physical assault on the liquor store clerk.

Several weeks after this occurrence, I went to the US marshal's office on another matter. As I walked by the holding cells, there was Alan with a cast and brace on his leg and his back to the cell door. He was telling all the other prisoners what had happened to him. I listened to him for a moment and yelled out his name. He turned his head, saw me, gave me a quick smile, and continued talking. I asked him how he was doing; he said fine, and we both acted as if nothing had happened between us.

At our next firearms-qualification session, the SAs scheduled to shoot that day met at our range north of Phoenix. Before actually stepping out to the range to qualify, we would come together and be given a classroom briefing on any new techniques, legal briefs, or anything that might arise to assist the SAs in their daily operations. Our firearms instructor, SA Jack Loughney, gathered everyone around to give a talk and, without any warning, told everyone to take a pen from their pocket, grip it in the strong hand, and jab forward in unison. Everyone complied. I did not as I immediately recognized what Jack was doing. He was looking at me from the corner of his eyes as I just shook my head. This would be our new attack mode in the event we happened to lose our weapon during a fight. I said, "Not funny, Jack," as everybody broke out into laughter. But I did appreciate the jab (pun intended) that Jack gave me. I expected no less, and Jack meant no harm. He was just having a fun moment with all of us, me in particular.

———◆———

SA Keith Tolhurst called a Desert Hawk task force conference to discuss the possible apprehension of a fugitive he was trying to locate with SA Steve Fillerup. A federal UFAP warrant was outstanding. Keith said that an investigation had determined that the fugitive was in Phoenix and out of money. He had apparently called a friend back east who was going to send him some money to help him out. These funds were being forwarded to a post-office service for the homeless and located in an area of town where the homeless could obtain a free meal sponsored by a religious organization.

Everyone could have family members or friends send them mail to this address; all they had to do was identify themselves, and they could retrieve their mail. From his investigation, Keith found out that the money would be arriving the next day, and it would be a great opportunity to apprehend his fugitive.

Keith and Steve set up an arrest plan using a large number of the team to set up surveillance and have an SA inside the facility to observe if the fugitive entered. That SA would then let everyone know when the person was there and provide a clothing description to all of us. Keith said that he and I would dress as homeless indigents and would wander around outside the facility, looking for this fugitive.

The following day, I came to work in dirty old Levi's and an old shirt. Both Keith and I bought a few tattoos from a hobby shop and put them on our arms. We tore our shirts a bit and rolled around in the garage area of the FBI compound to get some grease and dirt all over us. We looked disgusting. Keith said we could look realistic if I allowed him to urinate on me, so I could smell a bit. I drew the line there, and that did not happen.

We had backpacks with us that carried our FBI credentials, an FBI radio with an earpiece so it looked like an AM-FM radio, weapons, and handcuffs as well as other miscellaneous items such as crackers and water. One of the other units dropped us off several blocks from where the mail facility was located. We walked to that location and mingled with the other homeless people, who were waiting in line to eat when the food service opened up in several hours.

I estimated there had to be about a hundred people standing around, and we looked around for our fugitive but could not find him. So we mingled and talked with these homeless individuals, who were very kind to us. We told them we had just come in from El Paso and ridden a freight train to Phoenix, arriving just a short time earlier. They told us what time the meal line opened and praised the meal facility for what it offered. They also told us where we might find a place to sleep that night.

After a short period, we sat down on the sidewalk with our backs to a building; a few people told us that we were not allowed to sit down but had to remain standing. We ignored what they told us as we wanted to let them believe we could care less what the police wanted as long as we were not harming anyone.

After a short period, two police officers arrived on bicycles, driving through the crowd. They were both very pleasant to everyone, but the older one approached me, kicked at my foot, and told me that I had to stand as no sitting was allowed. I argued a bit, saying I had just arrived from El Paso and was drained. He stated that he could not help it, but he could not allow me to sit. So I stood up, grumbling, getting a dirty look from the officer. I can't say I blamed him as he was just doing his job and did not need any guff from some jerk looking for a free meal. The younger officer just stayed on his bike, waiting for the officer to finish with me, smiling at me, and telling me that he understood but they could not allow anyone to sit. Apparently, there was the belief that if everyone was allowed to sit, the facility became too backed up, and it made a real mess when everyone had to line up for the meal. I said I understood and told him I would not sit again. Both officers then left. At least we knew that our undercover ruse was working, and this minor confrontation with the police did not hurt any.

We waited around for another hour or so and talked with some more homeless people. Most of them were very likable, just down on their luck. I felt really sorry for them but realized there will always be people like them. As we talked, we felt like we had known them forever because they were so pleasant.

Just then the agent inside the facility announced over the FBI radios that the fugitive was inside and receiving his money. We had agreed earlier that we did not want to make any arrest inside the facility but would arrest him when he exited. The agent told us what the fugitive was wearing and said he could see no gun or bulge of any kind on his person.

The surveillance SAs moved up a bit, and Keith and I walked toward the door of the facility. The fugitive stepped outside, so Keith and I confronted him and arrested him on the spot. He was completely dumbfounded as it appeared he was being stopped by a couple of homeless people. Even more surprised were all the people to whom we had been talking earlier and who wondered what was going on.

After handcuffing the fugitive and handing him over to other team members to transport to jail, Keith and I started walking away but not before talking with all the new friends we had made on the street. They said that if they were ever arrested again, they wanted it to be by guys like Keith and me because we were so nice to them. Many of them came over and shook our hands as they now had a great story to tell all their other friends who were not there.

I will admit that ever since that day, I have developed a real respect for many of the homeless who just have had a hard time of it. God knows that a different turn or two in the road of life could put anyone there.

Of course, what Keith and I did became a topic of discussion among all our friends in the Phoenix Police Department robbery detail, with whom we worked extensively. We all got a laugh out of what had happened, especially with the two officers on the bicycles. When I told the story to the robbery detectives, I referred to the two officers as the nice guy and the jerk. He wasn't a jerk, but in my stupid way of telling the story, that is how I referred to him.

Several weeks later, I happened to be at the Phoenix police substation in south Phoenix doing some work, and who did I see but the officer who had kicked my shoe that day. Not thinking anything of it, I approached him and asked if he remembered me. He looked at me and shook his head. I then asked if he recalled us talking that day by the mail facility, and then he said he did and asked me if he was the nice guy or the jerk. Obviously, the story had gotten around with my crude remark, so I just laughed and said, "The jerk." He told me where to go and walked off. He was pretty upset, and I tried to explain it was just a term to separate one officer from the other, but he would have nothing further to say to me and just left. I felt bad about how dumb I was to use that term. I then asked a detective I knew who knew him personally to please explain my true intentions to him in using that word and that I did not mean anything by it.

I do not know if the detective ever told him this. But I do want to say that if you happen to be the officer who confronted me that day and may be reading this, I did not mean anything by it and now offer an apology for saying it.

Another lesson to be learned as life goes on.

Author and SA Keith Tolhurst dressing down
as homeless to locate fugitive

Temporary tattoo added to appear homeless

One of the most interesting arrests I was involved in was the arrest of a fugitive named Ronald Glyn Triplett, who was placed on the FBI's top-ten-most-wanted list. These fugitives are to be regarded as elusive and extremely dangerous. Any FBI office receiving information that a top-ten fugitive was in its territory dedicated unlimited resources to locate and arrest this person. Every FBI field office opens a case on every top-ten fugitive and assigns it to an SA to follow all prudent leads in an effort to locate and arrest the fugitive.

Triplett had escaped from a Michigan prison some three years before being placed on this list. He had been serving a lengthy sentence for attempted murder, armed robbery, and interstate flight. He was also wanted by New Mexico authorities for kidnapping, aggravated assault, sexual assault, and possession of stolen property, which had occurred after his escape from prison. Because of all his nefarious deeds, he met the requirements necessary to be placed on the most-wanted list.

This particular arrest occurred in May 1987 in Tempe, Arizona. Triplett had been investigated by the case agent in the Phoenix division, and the SA had developed information that there was a significant likelihood that he was living and working in the area. However, an exact location was not determined. The SA also learned there was a possibility that Triplett might be receiving a telephone call from a friend on a particular Saturday morning. This call would be coming in to a pay station located in a strip mall near Southern and Mill Avenues in Tempe. The time of the call could not be determined other than it was to be in the morning.

This information was brought to the attention of Special Agent in Charge Herb Hawkins, who called a conference on Friday to advise SAs of this information. He requested the FBI swat team be prepared to make the arrest if Triplett could be located the next day at this site. Other SAs, including me, were to be in the area in two-man units to conduct a discreet surveillance in the vicinity; if he was spotted, the SWAT team would move in and make the arrest. This tactic is the safest and most prudent way whenever a fugitive of this caliber is to be arrested. All circumstances of the surveillance/arrest were discussed and all options explored until a final plan was determined. Photographs of Triplett were distributed to everyone who would be working the case. Once I looked at the photo, my initial response was how closely he resembled a friend with whom I went to high school. The facial appearance was identical, and I knew that if I spotted Triplett, he would be easy to recognize.

On Saturday morning, all the SAs arrived early to designated locations in Tempe to begin watching all roads and parking lots in hopes of spotting

Triplett. He could have been living in adjoining apartment complexes or residential areas, so we watched those areas as well, ensuring to be extremely discreet so he would not spot the surveillance. The FBI SWAT team was positioned nearby to react if and when this dangerous fugitive was located.

As time went on and the morning hours approached the noon hour, it appeared that the information might not have been good since the call was to have been made in the morning and not in the afternoon. This information could have been inaccurate, and manpower would only be drained by staying out on the scene. Therefore, SAC Hawkins called a meeting with several SAs, the SWAT team leader, and the case agent. No new information was forthcoming, so Hawkins made a decision that we would break off the surveillance, and he directed the case agent to continue trying to develop more accurate information that might locate Triplett. Everyone was advised to break off but remain on standby in the event that additional information was forthcoming. This was a wise decision at the time. To continue the efforts on possibly erroneous information that could not be verified would only tire out the SAs and SWAT team, who might be needed at a later time to locate him and make the arrest.

SA Ron Myers asked SAC Hawkins if several SAs could stay around the area and continue the surveillance, and permission was granted. Myers contacted several of us, who volunteered to stay and work the area in hopes of Triplett showing up. Everyone else left, and about ten SAs remained. The SWAT team was released to return home. They would be called if we spotted Triplett. The ten remaining SAs got together and established parameters for the continuing surveillance. We broke off from this short meeting and proceeded to our designated locations.

The day continued with no results, and we all believed that the information about the telephone call had been inaccurate. Surveillances were extremely challenging and very dull as it got tiring watching cars and people in the area with no results. It was particularly difficult because this was happening near a very busy intersection in Tempe. Also, there were many pedestrians at the strip mall and many cars on adjoining streets and parking lots, and all of them only added to the stress of locating Triplett.

After several more hours, SA Myers broadcast on the FBI radio that he was in a shopping-center parking lot at the southwest corner of Mill and Southern. He further advised that a truck with a large camper shell had just parked nearby, and the person driving the truck was removing a motorcycle from the back of it. Myers was too far away from the person to identify him using binoculars, so he could not be positive who the person was. He was going to try to get closer to the individual, who was by then getting on the motorcycle and moving away from him, driving eastbound through the parking lot toward Mill Avenue.

I proceeded with my partner southbound on Mill toward his location, crossed Southern Avenue, and turned my blinkers on to turn right to enter this parking lot. As I made the turn, the person on the motorcycle drove up to Mill Avenue and started looking beyond me toward the street traffic, so he could enter Mill when there were no cars. I passed right by him and looked him straight in the face, and there was no question in my mind that this was either our fugitive or my friend with who I went to high school. It was uncanny to see him so closely resembling his photograph.

As I passed by him, I told my partner that it was Triplett and to advise all units that, in my opinion, this was our fugitive. Triplett was turning northbound onto Mill, and all units were scrambling to get in the area to see if they could see where he was going. We certainly did not want to get into a high-speed chase with him on a motorcycle as he would have the advantage in evading us. We advised everyone to be very discreet; if nothing else, if he did not detect the surveillance, he would be returning to this truck, and the arrest could be made at that time.

We all understood the necessity of being cautious so as not to alert Triplett. Fortunately, he came to a red light at Mill and Southern, and we were able to see him and easily get into position to follow him from a distance. As he proceeded northbound on Mill, he traveled for several blocks and then turned into a residential area.

Was he living at a home nearby? Did he always park his truck several blocks away and proceed home on motorcycle? These were questions we had no immediate answers for, but it was interesting that we were in the vicinity of where the telephone call would be coming to. At least we were in the right area and might be able to determine where he lived.

All of our radio traffic was being monitored by our personnel at the FBI field office. The dispatcher on duty asked if we wanted the SWAT team and the SAC notified, and we said that he should do this right away as we were certain we had the fugitive located, and he was not in custody.

I pulled my vehicle on the same street that Triplett turned on, but instead of turning east like he did, I turned west from Mill, drove a short distance, turned around, and parked facing east. We watched across the street to see if Triplett came back out on his motorcycle or if he might be on foot and visible to any of us. Other SAs moved in the area in discreet locations to assist. After a moment or two, Triplett came walking west-bound on the sidewalk and then turned left, walking south on the side-walk adjacent to Mill. He was at least several blocks away from the strip mall, walking slowly, and appeared at be at ease and not aware that he was being visually followed. I discreetly pulled my vehicle out onto the street and drove southbound on Mill until I came to the strip-mall entrance and then turned east into the strip mall. As I did this, other SAs could see me and advised all other SAs of what I was doing.

At this time, we made a decision that we would make the arrest since the SWAT team was en route but coming from the far north side of Phoenix, which was at least forty-five minutes away. We could not risk Triplett returning to his motorcycle and leaving the area when we had an excellent opportunity to arrest him.

A decision was made that my partner and I would get out of our car and go up to the window of the store on the west side of the mall that was facing Southern. We would just appear to look into the window at something we were interested in. If Triplett came to the steps of the sidewalk and turned east into the strip mall, we would be right there to make the arrest, and the SAs in the other cars were in the parking lot to assist. If Triplett continued walking southbound on the sidewalk, we would just come down a few steps once he passed us and get behind him. SA Myers would drive his vehicle, which was in the parking lot, to the street and intercept him, and we would all make the arrest.

As it happened, Triplett continued walking southbound, and as he passed about thirty feet west of us, we walked toward Mill and got behind him by about twenty feet. Immediately, SA Myers drove his vehicle to the street, slammed on his brakes, screeched to a halt, and came out with a shotgun, yelling, "FBI. You're under arrest." Triplett was completely stunned and fell backward right into my arms. I threw him to the ground, and my partner put a gun to his head. I just said, "FBI, Triplett. You're under arrest. Don't move, or you're dead." He was visibly shaken and said, "OK. I'm just glad it's over," or words to that effect. I then asked him, "You are Ron Triplett, aren't you?" He said he was. I was lying on his back as he lay facedown on the ground, and my partner assisted me in handcuffing him. Triplett was somewhat relieved as I am sure he thought he was going to be shot, and, I must admit, looking at SA Myers holding a shotgun was very menacing. Even though Myers held the barrel of the gun upward, Triplett had not known we were behind him, and he was shaken by all these events.

Once he was handcuffed and searched, we removed his wallet, which had his identification. We advised the office that Triplett was in custody and that they should notify the SAC and the SWAT team of this fact. We placed Triplett in the backseat of the FBI vehicle of the case agent, who would transport him to our office for fingerprinting, photographing, and interviewing.

Needless to say, all this action generated a considerable amount of attention from civilians and the general public. Traffic was backed up as we blocked off the entrance to the mall until we could safely resolve this entire matter and remove Triplett to our office. SAC Hawkins later came, and we filled him in on why we decided to make the arrest when we did rather than later, and he concurred with our decision.

During this entire time, Triplett was very congenial with us and pretty easygoing. I thought to myself that he did not seem like he was a very dangerous person and that he was likable in his own way. He was courteous and seemed to be glad that his time on the run, looking over his shoulder, was finally over.

Arriving at the FBI office, I went into the processing room to fingerprint and photograph Triplett. I then compared these fingerprints with those on the identification order that I had, and the prints were identical, verifying his identity. This IO was nothing more than the wanted poster we all observe in post offices throughout the country, containing the subject's photograph, description, legal information, and fingerprints. He did not resist in any way, but I could see that his mannerisms were now a bit different. He seemed to be angry and very upset that he had been arrested. This behavior was not unusual at all, but to see this change in such a short period concerned me. I mentioned this to other SAs, who could also see the change in his disposition. We just wanted to make sure that we did not ease up, giving him the opportunity to assault or try to escape from us. We kept it strictly professional but direct, and it was evident to him that the only place he was going was to the Maricopa County jail. He later relaxed again.

Shortly after that, as we sat there talking following a brief interview, one of the other SAs brought me the top-ten wanted poster that had Triplett's photo and description on it. Triplett looked at it and mentioned that he made "the big time." He then looked at it again, smiled, and asked to borrow a pen. He signed his name, dated it "5/16/87," and noted, GOOD LUCK, with his initials underneath. I asked him what that meant, and he said that he was sincere in its meaning as we had treated him professionally during this entire arrest. I still have this wanted poster today as a memento and reminder of this arrest.

———◆———

One of the wildest chases I have ever been involved in started with a telephone call one early morning from the Kansas City division. The SA told me they were conducting surveillance of a fugitive named Donald, a bank robber wanted in their division. However, the problem was that the fugitive had a brother who looked identical, and he lived in Phoenix. The person they had under surveillance had just boarded an airplane for Phoenix with an undercover SA boarding behind him to keep him under constant surveillance. They were not sure if this person was the fugitive or the brother and did not want to take any action unless they were positive of who he was. If it was the wrong person, the fugitive would go deeper into hiding.

I immediately thought, Why me? Every time I worked a criminal case from someone from the Kansas City division, it resulted in a violent solution. We had a shooting, a physical fight, or high-speed chases resulting in crashes. And now I was getting another one.

I told the SA that I would get a group of SAs and detectives and go to the airport to see if we could resolve the matter. The SA provided all the specifics about this person and what time the plane was due to arrive in Phoenix. Thankfully, we had several hours to prepare and plan.

I called several SAs together and then contacted a sergeant at the robbery detail of the PXPD, who would get us some more manpower from the PD. We went to the airport to await the flight. Also, we sent a few SAs to the brother's residence to watch the house. Once we could view this person at the airport, we would have the SAs go to the house and knock on the door to see if the brother was at home. If he was, we then knew this person at the airport would be the fugitive. If no one was home, we would still be at square one, not knowing if this was the fugitive or the brother. We just had to bide our time.

Several hours later, the flight arrived, and a person resembling the fugitive came walking out of the terminal followed by an individual who had been earlier described to us as the SA from the Kansas City division. He hooked up with our SAs as we maintained the surveillance and watched Donald get into a van driven by a young female. He took over driving as he got into the van and drove away from the airport.

Fortunately, we had about eight vehicles to follow him, and these cars were occupied by veteran SAs and PXPD detectives. We worked on a dedicated channel with the PD, so we could all hear the direction of this moving surveillance.

In the meantime, the SAs were able to locate the brother at his residence in Phoenix, so we were now certain that the person driving the van was Donald, our fugitive. We continued the moving surveillance, not wanting to make a felony stop on the information we had, specifically that this person was extremely dangerous and did not want to go back to jail. We had sufficient surveillance units without being spotted, and the surveillance worked well for a period of time.

As this van approached a shopping center parking lot near Nineteenth Avenue and Bethany Home Road, it pulled into the lot and parked near a bank. Great, I thought—don't tell me that this guy just got to Phoenix and is going to rob a bank. (Actually, we later learned that the woman had to go to the bathroom, and they had a small portable potty in the van; they stopped so she could use it. How many times does this happen? But it happened in this case.)

Since we were not sure what they were up to, we thought this was a very good time to surround the van with our surveillance units and block them in. We could then make the arrest. As some of our units closed in, Donald, who was obviously paranoid, spotted one of them and immediately sped away before our blocking car could get into position. The blocking car missed getting into position by merely a few feet, but the van was able to slide away from the vehicles closing in, and the chase was on.

I was driving a car with the sergeant from the PXPD in the passenger seat. The van was northbound in the parking lot, and I was on the street north of him, driving eastbound. I saw him approaching the end of the parking lot as the van jumped a few bushes and the sidewalk and went onto the same street I was on. He drove right in front of me and turned westbound at high speed. I made a quick U-turn and got behind him, turning on my siren and placing an emergency revolving light on the dashboard. I watched as the sergeant hooked up his seatbelt; I am sure he thought he was going for a wild ride. He was right—we were.

The van was passing other cars like they were standing still. The sergeant got permission from his headquarters to broadcast our position and direct the chase on the radio. We were going around cars and through small parking lots, and this maniac in the van didn't care about any harm he could cause anyone. I was on his tail and was hoping he knew he would not get away and would surrender. How wrong I was.

He drove toward the freeway on a side street, and when he arrived at the frontage road, instead of turning right to get on the frontage road and onto the freeway, he turned left and went south against traffic on the frontage road. I held back a bit as I could see all I was doing was making him take chances. He turned off the frontage road going eastbound and drove around surface streets, being picked up by marked police units and surveillance units alike. At one point, he came to a complete stop, and I thought he would get out of his van and either surrender or shoot it out with us. I got out of my car with my gun drawn, and as I did, he started up again and sped away. Here we go again.

After another minute or so, he drove this van near the exterior of an underground parking lot and got out with his gun, pointing it at a few SAs as he ran down the ramp and entered this parking lot.

One SA named Mike McComas had joined this chase with SA Susan Stamper when Donald drove the van toward this underground parking lot. As Donald exited his van, Mike got out of the FBI car driven by SA Stamper so that he could confront the fugitive. Donald was running down the south-side down ramp of the parking lot as the SA from Kansas City shot at him but just missed him as he dove behind a concrete barrier. The driver had abandoned his girlfriend in the van, and she was immediately arrested by a few police officers, and the van was secured. SA McComas chased Donald down into the underground parking lot, where the subject hijacked a small sports car from a female driver and drove away. SA McComas came back out of the parking lot to get into his vehicle to follow him and report what happened. However, SA Stamper drove around to the other side of the parking lot to cut off the fugitive if he came out. SA McComas could not find the car SA Stamper was driving but saw another SA, Gary Reinecke, and jumped into the car with him to try to find this violent and desperate fugitive who had driven off.

As this was happening, I parked my car next to another ramp near the east side of the garage, an obvious exit. The sergeant ran toward the south garage entry, and I took the other ramp on the east side. As I was running down this east ramp, a small sports car came shooting up it. I yelled at the driver, initially not realizing that it was Donald. As he passed, he swerved at me, but I jumped to a small sidewalk next to the ramp, and he did not hit me.

I immediately radioed the description of this sports car and his direction of travel. Other officers down in the garage found the young lady who was the victim of this carjacking and obtained additional information from her. She was petrified but not physically harmed except for having been forcibly pulled from her car.

I ran back to my car and started driving up the street where I had last seen the sports car leaving. It was a major street, and there was a number of cars on the road. I drove north and east and then south and west, not knowing where I was going but just hoping I would see the car. The sergeant was no longer with me as he was still back at the garage.

I was furious with myself. How in the hell could I let this guy get away? We had him surrounded, and he managed to escape. But given his frantic nature of a trapped animal, it is not hard to imagine how he might escape. I did not blame anyone but myself as it was I who had made the call to make the arrest in the parking lot. It was I who had continued the chase, and it was I who had lost this man. At least I felt this way. I was just hoping he would not later take a hostage and kill somebody.

Radio traffic was thinning out as no leads were coming in as to where this person could be. Ten minutes went by, but it felt like hours. I hit the steering wheel, really upset with myself for losing this fugitive.

Then I heard a police radio broadcast from the PXPD helicopter advising that the vehicle was southbound on a major street in west Phoenix. Two SAs were en route to this location, as were other vehicles. The driver of one car, SA Gary Reinecke, who had SA McComas with him, saw a PXPD detective he recognized standing on the side of the road, and his car appeared to be disabled. SA Reinecke skidded to a stop and told the detective to get in the backseat. Reinecke then continued to the location where the fugitive appeared to be heading in the hope of cutting him off.

As they approached a major intersection in west Phoenix, SAs Reinecke and McComas spotted the fugitive in the sports car driving south into the intersection at high speed. Reinecke looked at McComas, who nodded, and Gary made an immediate decision, sped up the FBI car, and rammed the sports car on the driver's side, causing it to veer into a spin and come to a complete stop, receiving substantial and severe damage. The fugitive tried to put the car in gear and drive away, but there was too much damage, and the car wouldn't move. Donald then reached down for his gun and started raising it but changed his mind as he looked up and saw SA McComas and SA Reinecke out of the FBI car and pointing their guns, locked and loaded, at this head. Donald dropped his gun and was immediately placed under arrest.

It was very ironic that SA McComas had been one of the first SAs to confront Donald and almost make the initial arrest back in the parking garage only to later locate him again and, with SA Reinecke, stop him by ramming his car and subsequently make the arrest. These were two great SAs staying in the fight and not giving up, resulting in the end of a very dangerous chase and the arrest of a very dangerous, elusive, and desperate fugitive.

Finally, it was over. Nobody was killed, and there were just a few minor injuries. There were some damaged vehicles, and reports would have to be written about this entire incident. But Donald was going to jail.

Donald was taken to the FBI office for fingerprints and photographs. We had four of our biggest SAs standing with him since he was a weightlifter. He had massive arms and was extremely fit. He started cooperating, deciding it was over and that he would not want to fight the huge SAs standing round him. We then got the fingerprints and photographs.

After a short time, an SA came to me and said he had conducted a little background on this fugitive and believed he had come up with a residence on the west side of Phoenix where Donald was possibly living. This residence was not too far from where the arrest had taken place, and we believed he might have been returning home to hide. I thought it might be prudent to get a search warrant for this residence. This attempt to get one took several hours, and while others took Donald to the US marshal's office for a hearing before a federal judge, I and several others went to the residence to conduct the search. What a treasure chest we found. We located money that we were able to trace to a bank robbed in Kansas City. Also, we found several more guns, one of them a "street sweeper," a twelve-gauge shotgun with a rotating magazine holding twelve rounds; it was an extremely dangerous weapon.

This case started early in the morning, and I did not get home until about ten that night. I was extremely tired, my adrenalin was still up, and I had a hard time going to sleep.

Donald was returned to Kansas City, where he went to trial for the bank robberies he was involved in, was convicted, and received a substantial time in prison.

Why did I know that morning when the call came from Kansas City that it was going to be an adventure? It always seemed to happen on Kansas City calls, and it sure did that day when Donald came to town.

———————

After leaving the FBI Training Academy in Quantico, Virginia, I was sent to my first office in Columbia, South Carolina. As a first-office agent (FOA), I had virtually no experience in working criminal cases but was accepted as someone who could be counted on to perform anything that was expected of me. I was assigned to an experienced SA named Dick Oyler, who led me through the tedious paperwork expected of all SAs as well as worked cases with me and answered the endless questions I had.

He made sure I was doing all the right things so that when I was released to work on my own, I could handle all investigations handed over to me. One of the most unusual arrests I was involved in happened there in South Carolina.

Two fugitives were said to be heading our way from the State of Louisiana, where they had taken part in a bank robbery in which a police officer was brutally shot at point-blank range and left to die. The case was given high priority in Columbia, and several SAs were working on it together with instructions to use whatever manpower was needed to find and arrest these two extremely dangerous fugitives.

The investigation determined that the men were staying at two separate cabins at Lake Murray, a recreational area about thirty-five miles west of Columbia. Several SAs were out there trying to find the two cabins, and the rest of the SAs were gathered in the office for an all-agent conference. We were all informed of the investigation results and of the fact that the two cabins had been located. Since it was late evening, the case agent thought it best to make the arrests in the early-morning hours, when the fugitives were most likely asleep. The cabins were being watched by some SAs in the event that the fugitives might leave during the night, but there was no information that suggested that would happen. We were told to go home, get a few hours' rest, and report to the office and be ready to leave by 3:00 a.m. for the drive to the cabins. Teams were being developed, and assignments would be given to us the next morning when we came to the office.

When I arrived, I was assigned to ride with SA Jim Calhoun, a huge man who lived on a ranch outside of Columbia with his wife, their children, and several horses. He had grown up in Winslow, Arizona, and we had a lot in common since we had both grown up in the West. Jim stood about six feet four and weighed at least a solid 220 pounds. We were like a *Mutt and Jeff* team when we stood together, but that did not bother me in the least as I got to know him as a friend as well as a colleague.

We drove out to Lake Murray in some units and met at a designated location upon arriving there. We were met at this site by one of the SAs who had stayed out there all night keeping watch on the cabins, which were near each other. He drew out a schematic that designated which fugitive was located in which cabin. The SAC said that at daybreak, we would go to the first cabin and announce our presence, telling the fugitive to surrender as he was surrounded by the FBI. As we did this, other SAs would be covering the other cabin, making sure that fugitive would not escape or interfere with the other arrest.

At daybreak, it was announced that we would make the first arrest. Jim and I were stationed about fifty feet away and covered by a large tree. The SA making the announcement had a bullhorn and made the announcement as he had been instructed. Nothing happened. He made the announcement again, and shortly after that, we could see a curtain move. The SA told the person to come out and that he would not be hurt. We could hear the person say something to the effect that he was coming out and not to shoot; he said he was unarmed. Just then the door opened, and out walked this man with his hands raised over his head. He was completely nude. He turned around as instructed, and I guess he just wanted to take no chances; he made sure we knew he had no weapons on him.

Now, you have to imagine this. It was in the middle of winter; there was snow on the ground, and here was this man, completely nude and shivering from the cold. I certainly did not want to give him my coat and freeze, and no one else did either. He was told to get down on his knees, and he complied.

At this time, the announcement was made to the person in the other cabin. We got no response whatsoever—no moving curtains, no verbal response, nothing. Several efforts were made to get his attention, and we could not imagine that he could not hear us, but he was not responding.

Jim looked at me and told me he'd had enough of this. He told everyone to hold their fire as we were going to approach the cabin. But before we did, Jim and I walked over to the fugitive kneeling down, and Jim lifted him up and walked him in front of us as we approached the other cabin. We walked right up to the door, and Jim started pounding on it, yelling, "FBI!" and telling the other fugitive to come out. Within a moment or so, a sleepy-eyed man came to the door, saw his partner standing there nude with his hands in the air, and started laughing. He thought his buddy must be playing a joke on him. Then he saw us with our weapons drawn and immediately raised his hands and surrendered. As we grabbed hold of him, other SAs came forward to help in the arrest. We transported them back to Columbia for an appearance before the US magistrate, and they were later returned to Louisiana to stand trial for the bank robbery and shooting of the officer.

I had to hand it to Jim. He was not one who wasted any time, and he took advantage of a situation whenever it presented itself. Perhaps we could be criticized for doing what we did, but in the final analysis, no one got hurt, and both fugitives went to jail.

———◆———

When the Desert Hawk fugitive task force was formed, many new friendships and associations were developed, and we all occasionally came together to socialize outside of work. We had several cookouts, luncheons, and so on, and we decided to form a men's softball league. Although we were not an outstanding team, we had great times going out and competing against other teams and just getting together with each other outside of work.

One evening after a game, Dave Schumenski, a detective from the PXPD and a member of our task force, told us he had a case on a fugitive who was extremely elusive and most certainly would run if confronted by the police. The softball field we were playing on was a short distance from a residence where this fugitive could have been temporarily residing. It was a long shot, but Dave asked all of us if we could help him for a short time while he led a brief surveillance on the residence. We all agreed, so at about 9:00 p.m., following the softball game, we left for this residence. Dave gave us several photos he had of the fugitive and provided us with all the descriptive details that he had.

Across the street from the residence was a large empty field full of tall weeds. It was great cover for anyone who wanted to crawl through the weeds to get a good view of the house. Danny Snodgrass and I said we would set up in the field, so we got on our hands and knees and crawled through the field with a pair of binoculars and our radios. Once we reached a sufficient position for a decent view of the house, we radioed to the others that we could see into the house through a large picture window with sheer drapes. We saw a man walking back and forth on occasion but could not identify that person because of the curtains.

Dave said that the best information he had was that there was no one living at this residence, so this could be his fugitive. We had no way to confirm if this man was the subject, so we asked Dave to speed down the street and squeal his tires, hopefully getting the person to look out and give us the opportunity to get a better view of him.

Dave did this, driving down the street, slamming on his brakes, and making a loud squeal with his tires. Sure enough, the person came over to the window, opened the curtains a bit, and looked out. He looked like the fugitive, but we could not make any clear identification. What we could say for certain was that the person appeared to be very jittery. Dave suggested to one of the team members that he walk up near the house and find a place to hide in the event the person came outside. Then we might be able to make a better identification and even an arrest if he was the fugitive and the opportunity presented itself.

Dave did not want to risk just going up to the house to confront the person because if this man was not the fugitive, we would have blown the lead he had about this residence; that could alert the fugitive to what Dave had determined from his investigation. Therefore, one of the team members casually walked up near the house and disappeared into a gigantic bush just outside of a tall cinder-block wall that surrounded the entire yard.

After about fifteen minutes, that team member saw a lone male come out of the side gate, walking fast down the street. Dave suggested that we wait until the person was about a block away and then try to identify him. The team member in the bush came out and started to follow the subject on foot, and one of the other cars pulled up near the fugitive with the intent of getting out to talk to him. When this happened, the unidentified male started running as fast as he could. The person following him yelled into the radio that the man running was the fugitive we were seeking. Dave contacted the PXPD on another radio he had and requested assistance in locating this individual. The fugitive jumped a fence into a backyard, and all we could do at this time was form a perimeter in the area to prevent him from breeching it and escaping.

Within minutes, numerous PXPD marked units infiltrated the area and helped in maintaining the perimeter. A PXPD helicopter came in to assist, and a requested canine unit responded. A gradual search was started to minimize the controlled area, and the perimeter was shortened. It was a methodical search, and after about an hour, we were able to compress the area from about three square blocks to about one square block.

I was in a car with Danny and watched as a canine and his handler went from door to door looking for the fugitive. We were about 150 feet from one house when we heard the canine handler advise the helicopter on the police radio to hover over the house he was at as the canine was alerting him to the fact that the person could be on the roof. The helicopter flew over the house with the search lights off; when he got to the house, he turned the lights on. The house was flooded from above with a bright light, and I could see the fugitive jump up from the roof where he had been lying and leap into the backyard. I then looked down and watched the officer run into the backyard through a gate on the side. My immediate thought was that this officer was alone with the subject, so I jumped out of the car and sprinted to the gate. I heard Danny yelling something but could not understand what he was saying because of the loud noise of the helicopter. So I kept running, and once I entered the yard, I could see the fugitive running on the far side of an underground swimming pool. He was running to the fence, and I yelled at him to stop. He kept running, so I darted to my right and ran at him. Just as he was jumping to the top of the tall fence, I jumped at him and took him to the ground. He fell, and I landed on top of him as he started yelling and screaming. You would have thought I had broken his arm or leg, as loud as he was. I had to admit that I thought this old boy (me) still had a bit of life in him and could handle his own. He kept screaming, and then I actually started thinking what I had done to this guy; all I wanted to do was stop and subdue him, and now I was somehow hurting him.

I just told him to quiet down as I wrestled with him to get him hand-cuffed. Then I realized there were some officers around, helping to subdue this fugitive. I then noticed that the canine had the fugitive by his leg and was gnawing at him with his sharp fangs. The handler was pulling the canine away, and, once he removed him, the fugitive stopped yelling. We got him handcuffed, and an officer escorted him out to the front of the house.

Hmm, I guess it was not I who was hurting the guy; it was this canine, who had a death grip on his leg just above his knee and who was pulling him away as I held him to the ground. And all that time I thought that this guy was a real wimp and that I was the stud. But then reality came into play, and I learned the truth. The canine was the real stud.

What I had not realized earlier was that the officer had released the canine into the backyard before running there himself. I was watching the fugitive jump from the roof into the backyard as the dog apparently went in through the gate. I did not see the dog go into the backyard. I also did not conclude that the reason the fugitive was running was because the dog was giving chase. There was no need for me to even approach the fugitive as the canine would have done the job for us.

Danny had been yelling that I should back off as the canine and the handler would subdue the fugitive. If I had been able to hear him, I certainly would have backed off, but my concern at the time was for what I believed was the lone officer in the backyard with the fugitive.

After a few minutes, a PXPD supervisor came up to me and said that the policy of the PXPD was to let the canine and handlers make the arrest of the subject for the sake of safety. He was very congenial but direct, and I told him that I had thought the officer was alone and might need assistance. He said he understood my position and that I was fortunate that the canine had grasped on to fugitive's leg and not mine. The dog could not differentiate between legs and merely went after one of them; it could have been my leg that was receiving attention from paramedics.

I immediately approached the canine handler and apologized for interfering in the arrest. He just smiled and said there was no problem and he was just happy that I was the one who did not get bit. He went on to explain that once a police dog is let loose, the officer will allow it to take the fugitive down until other officers and the handler arrive and relieve the canine. There have been many instances where some officers got too close to the arrest, and the canine latched on to their legs, resulting in severe bites requiring medical attention. I really understood the gravity of this and thanked him and his canine for their assistance.

This officer and his supervisor were extremely professional in how they handled the matter, and I was grateful for that. This issue was brought to the attention of all the other team members, some of whom did not know the policy of the PXPD regarding canines and their handlers.

I then went over to Danny and told him about this issue, and he said he was aware of it and thought that I knew about it. He said that as I got out of the car to assist the officer, he was yelling at me to come back and let the canine handle it, but I just kept running. I told him I could not hear him, and he said that he followed me at a distance but stayed back when he saw the dog jump in and grab the fugitive by the leg. He just smiled and said it was a good thing it was not my leg.

I looked over to where the fugitive was sitting handcuffed on the street by a police car. Danny said he was having a marked police unit transfer the guy to jail, and the officer would book him. I walked over to where the fugitive was sitting on the ground by himself with several officers standing a short distance away. As I got closer, I realized why this was happening.

When the canine had grabbed the guy's leg, he had defecated in his pants, and the stench was unbearable. I went back to Danny with a smirk on my face to tell him this, and he said that was the reason he had asked another officer to transfer him to jail. In fact, he had found a rookie and asked him how long he had been on the job, and this rookie said it was his first week. Danny asked if would like to transfer the fugitive to jail and book him in for the task force, and the rookie said he would. Then Danny handed him over to the rookie officer, who immediately became a bit perplexed about the stench. He asked Danny what he should do, and Danny said just to put him in his car and drive him downtown as fast as he could. He might consider breathing through his mouth as well. The rookie was not too happy.

I learned a valuable lesson about working with the canine unit, and after seeing the bite on the fugitive's leg, there is no way I would ever wish that on anyone I knew.

After critiquing this arrest the following day, I announced my appreciation of the canine unit of the PXPD and further instructed all members of our team that if we ever used this unit in the future, we'd let them take the lead and have them tell us what they wanted from us.

I also learned that when chasing fugitives, do not be surprised at all the *crap* you will get, literally.

CHAPTER 3
Kidnappings

———◆———

THERE ARE MANY CASES THAT FBI SAs work that fill their daily lives with extreme emotions. These cases can range from complete elation, such as the recovery of a kidnapped child who is returned unharmed to the grieving parents and relatives, to devastating sorrow when events lead to harm or death to the victims. Either way, we must do all we can to remain as calm as possible so as to complete our investigations logically and not be controlled by any emotional reasoning. If not, we could taint our investigations in the eyes of the legal profession because our results have been driven by our emotions.

The FBI becomes involved in a potential kidnapping of any person if the information received claims that the individual was taken against his or her own free will. As a rule, the person must be transported across a state line to make this a federal offense, but many times it is not known if the person has crossed the state line. The FBI will continue to work the case regardless because of a twenty-four presumptive clause, which means that once twenty-fours have elapsed, the FBI can assume that the person was transported across state lines. If we work the case, we will work jointly with local agencies, and if we determine that the individual was never transported across a state line, the local jurisdiction will become the lead agency and assume prosecutorial discretion. The FBI will turn over all evidence collected and all statements about the case to the local prosecutor for future prosecution.

———————

Such was the case I worked in 1983, the detention and murders of US Marine Corps Captain Robert Bravence and his wife, Cheryl.

It was June, and I was sitting at my desk, working on some paperwork for another case. The SA taking criminal complaints from the general public came and told me that he had just received a telephone call from a lady named Gilda Howard, who said that her son and daughter-in-law were missing. He said that normally this would just be referred to local authorities, but there was something about this case that just did not seem right, and he asked me if I would call and talk to her to see what I thought. He then gave me her telephone number.

I phoned Ms. Howard to get some information, and she related the following, as close as I can recall. Her son, Robert Bravence, was a captain in the USMC and was temporarily stationed in El Paso, Texas, as an instructor to other military personnel. He and his wife, Cheryl, were going to take a small trip up to northern Idaho to do some hiking and mountain climbing. Both were very adventurous and athletic, and they loved the outdoors and this type of activity. Robert told her that on their return trip to El Paso, they would stop and visit with her for a day or two in Scottsdale before continuing to El Paso.

She said she had expected them to come on the previous Friday and then on Saturday when they did not show up on Friday. On Sunday, she had become very concerned because this was not like her son. He was always concerned about her welfare and would never cause her to worry about him. If he was running late, he would have contacted her, but she had heard nothing and was genuinely afraid that something might have happened to him and Cheryl.

Something was not right, so I told her that I wanted to come to her home to get everything in detail so that I could follow up on this. I told the SA to open up an FBI complaint form listing the necessary information, take it to the supervisor, and have him open and assign the case to me, designating it as a kidnapping. I was going to Scottsdale to talk with Ms. Howard.

The information allowed me to have this case opened as a potential kidnapping case under Title 18, US Code, Section 1201. The FBI will work these violations under the Federal Kidnapping Statute, which allows investigative entry if anyone is transported across state lines for ransom or otherwise. In this case, we were unsure if there had been a kidnapping, but the possibility existed. The twenty-four-hour presumptive clause contained in this statute allowed us to investigate even though we were uncertain of the events. The fact that the potential victims in this case had not made contact with anyone led me to believe that they had been prevented from doing so and possibly could have been abducted.

I arrived at the residence of Ms. Howard and talked with her for several hours, noting the last time she'd had contact with her son as well as the names of any of his associates in and out of the military, his immediate supervisor in El Paso, and his wife's relatives. She said she had already talked with Cheryl's parents, and they had not heard from them either. She gave me their address and telephone number so that I could dispatch SAs to interview them at length.

After gathering all this information, I sent out a teletype to FBI HQ in Washington, DC, all West Coast offices, the field office where Cheryl's parents lived, the field offices in El Paso, and every office jurisdiction they might have traveled through to get to Idaho. I provided all of them with the information I had gathered and set out specific leads for several of these offices. Some of the other offices not getting specific leads were notified in the event they happened to come across any information of value. Campgrounds in every state were checked to see if this young couple had perhaps stayed at one of them, but this all met with negative results. Everything that could be done was being done, but we were striking out.

Although I knew nothing specific, I had a terrible gut feeling that something had happened to this couple, but when or where it had happened was a mystery. I told Ms. Howard what I was doing in my investigation and that I would keep her apprised of anything that developed. Hopefully, we could find her son and daughter-in-law. She said that if they contacted her or she learned anything, she would immediately notify me.

This initial inquiry resulted in nothing more than determining when they had left El Paso for their trip. The SA working in El Paso secured information such as credit-card and banking records. He also obtained Robert's and Cheryl's dental charts in the event they were needed to make any identification.

I took the information about the credit cards and placed stops with the credit-card company to immediately notify the FBI if any charges appeared. I stayed in daily contact with Ms. Howard. Several days later, she called and told me that she had received information from the base in El Paso. The Los Angeles Police Department had told them that a van belonging to Robert Bravence had been found abandoned in Los Angeles. I immediately telephoned a good friend at the FBI office there who worked reactive cases and asked him to contact the LAPD and get the specifics about this abandoned van.

Ralph did a superb job not only getting the information but also going to the location of the van and helping to search it thoroughly. There was little evidence in the van, but some latent fingerprints were taken, and the van had some spent shotgun shells in the rear portion that he confiscated and preserved for any future prosecution.

We now knew that the vehicle that was last seen in El Paso was now in Los Angeles with the possibility of it having been driven through New Mexico, Colorado, Utah, Idaho, Oregon, and Washington State. At least we had some direction going forward and would now be doing more investigation to resolve this matter.

I notified Ms. Howard that we were working hard on this case, and this sweet woman, who was terrified beyond belief, was cordial and extremely patient with me. I would see her at her residence to brief her on any developments, and she always treated me with undue respect. I knew the day would come when she would become exasperated with the investigation and lack of immediate results. Although we were developing leads to investigate, her son and Cheryl were still missing. She feared the worst but hoped for the best.

Eventually, the credit-card company started notifying us of the usage of the cards, and we set out specific leads for motels, restaurants, gas stations, and anywhere else the card charges directed us. The information we were getting was that two males were using the card. On several motel-registration forms, they would scribble a name and put an address that we immediately would check out without any positive results. The interesting thing was that all these registration forms noted several cities in Texas. The street names were accurate but not necessarily coming from the listed city. For example, a street name on one form for the city of Dallas was not in Dallas but in Houston. This happened several times, but all the addresses were in Texas. The scribbled names that the suspects used were common ones, and we gained nothing of value from them.

June turned into July, July into August, and leads were slowing up. Nothing seemed to be accomplished, and the credit-card information stopped completely. Apparently, the kidnappers got rid of the cards after using them on this trip and did not want anything that could be used to track them further.

I stayed in contact with Ms. Howard, who was starting to feel the strain. One day, she called and screamed at me over the telephone. I had known this day would come, and I could hardly blame her. The FBI was the one hope she had in finding her Robert and Cheryl, and I did not bring them back. I was a father and completely understood her passion and emotion. I tried to calm her, and eventually she did calm down and apologize to me. I told her no apology was necessary as I completely appreciated and understood what she was going through. She was entirely correct in how she felt, and I expected nothing otherwise.

As time went on, I became completely frustrated at the lack of progress and had a hard time going to sleep each night as I was constantly wondering what else could be done to find this young couple. I became angry at my lack of success and hated going to work, knowing that I would have to tell Ms. Howard we had nothing new but were all still working on it. She was the most compassionate person I had ever met. She held no animosity toward me or the FBI, knowing fully well we were doing all we could. Nevertheless, her son and daughter-in-law were still missing.

In addition to Ms. Howard, I maintained contact with a representative from the USMC. This upstanding marine would always call to determine if we had made any substantial progress or if he could help in any way. I was under tremendous pressure as I was starting to realize that unless we got more information or developments, this case might never be solved. But the pressure I had was nothing compared to what that poor mother was going through. I told myself I would never give up in this case, no matter how long it took, and daily committed myself to finding this couple.

Then one September night, I woke up at about one in the morning to a ringing telephone. The FBI SA in Idaho who was working the case told me that he believed the remains of Robert and Cheryl had been found. A couple of hunters found some remains and notified local authorities, who contacted the FBI. He was currently getting ready to drive out to meet up with the law-enforcement personnel who were standing by, and, from what he had learned from them already, there was no question these remains were those of the young couple. I told him that if he was positive, I would notify Ms. Howard. He said that would be proper; he was positive of the findings, and there was no question in his mind that the remains of the young couple had been located.

I contacted our office in Phoenix and asked the person on duty to contact the SAs where Cheryl's parents lived so that they could notify them. I then contacted the USMC representative, told him that I was going to make the death notification, and asked him if he would be present. He said he would go with me, so I met him at designated area, and he followed me in his car to Ms. Howard's house.

Arriving at her home, I rang the doorbell, and she came to the door, asking who it was. I told her, and she opened the door and invited the

USMC officer and me into her house. Her eyes teared up as I believe she knew what I was going to tell her. Why else would I be there at such an early-morning hour? I just told her that we had found her son and Cheryl, and they were no longer with us. I cannot recall the exact words as this was one of the hardest things I ever had to do, but I recognized that it needed to come from me. She stood proudly and asked if we would excuse her for a moment or two, and then she walked to another room, where I could hear her crying. I looked up at the USMC officer, who, like me, had tears in his eyes as he remained tall, firm, and proud.

Ms. Howard returned to the room wiping her eyes, asked us to sit down, and inquired if we wanted something to drink. We declined, and she asked us to tell her what information we had for her. I told her what I knew, which was somewhat limited, and that we were on our way to finding out what had happened and solving this case. When I developed more information, she would be advised. She said that all she wanted was to get her children back so that she would be able to give them a proper burial. What a grand and dignified woman. She was suffering such pain, but she was able to come to terms with this tragedy and only wanted to have her loved ones returned for a proper burial.

I stayed for a short time and then left as I needed to get back to find out what the Idaho SA had learned and what needed to be done to find the criminals who had committed this awful crime. The USMC officer told me that he would remain with Ms. Howard and would ensure that someone from the USMC would be with her at her residence or immediately outside at all times until her loved ones were put to rest. They would be there for her and for anything she needed, and they were, from that moment on until the day this young couple was buried. Someone from the USMC was always around, standing by this great woman. I still hold them in the highest regard for how they treat their own to make sure they will always remain a family.

Once the remains of Robert Bravence and his wife were located, a crime-scene investigation was conducted by the FBI and local authorities. Their remains were located in a wooded area and covered by dense brush and limbs and were very difficult to spot. The investigators and FBI SAs conducting the crime-scene investigation taped off the entire area. Also, they looked far beyond the area where the remains were located and spotted an abandoned car that had also been covered with bush and tree limbs. It was extremely difficult to spot, but their tenacity and professionalism in the investigation allowed them to locate it.

A search of this vehicle revealed some interesting pieces of evidence, some of which included the names of two individuals, Mark and Bryan Lankford. Both of them were from Texas. Finally, we were on to something.

The possibility now existed that this young couple perhaps had been confronted at this location by these two men, who wanted their vehicle as apparently something was wrong with the one they abandoned. They killed the young couple, took their van, and traveled in it, abandoning it in Los Angeles, California. The realization that this scenario occurred at this site removed the possibility that the young couple was kidnapped and transported across a state line. In essence, the FBI would probably lose jurisdiction, and all information would now be turned over to authorities in Idaho as they opened a murder case. The two men became prime suspects. However, the FBI was still allowed to assist these agencies with out-of-state leads that needed to be conducted, and we did not close our case but proceeded all the more aggressively.

Now that we had suspects, we were able to obtain information about them. We were eventually able to confirm that the latent fingerprints on the abandoned van in California matched these men. Also the handwriting on lodging, food, and gas receipts came back as positive matches. The evidence was stacking up.

In October 1983, Mark and Bryan Lankford were both located camping near the Trinity River in Texas, and both were placed under arrest for the murders of Robert and Cheryl Bravence. Evidence collected at this site consisted of property belonging to Robert Bravence that was then in the possession of these men. All this evidence was used to convict them during their subsequent trial.

Both men went to trial in Idaho for the murders, both were found guilty, and both received the verdict of a death penalty. Over the course of some twenty years, each blamed the other for the deaths of this young couple, but the courts upheld the convictions for both. Eventually, both men were removed from death row and sentenced to serve life terms for this crime.

It was a long and complicated battle of appeals, hearings, continued appeals, and so on. The last decision was that Mark Lankford had been sentenced to two life terms without the possibility of parole, and Bryan Lankford was sentenced to a single life term with the possibility of parole and release from prison in 2018.

When the remains of Robert and Cheryl Bravence were returned to Arizona, I received a telephone call from Ms. Howard. She said that they were to be buried in Scottsdale together and asked if I would attend the funeral. I told her I would be honored. She gave me the date and time, and I told her I would be there.

I attended this service in the very early morning of a frigid day. The service in Scottsdale was being held jointly with a memorial service in El Paso, Texas, to honor Captain Bravence and his wife at the base where he had been stationed. Since the service was at 6:00 a.m. in El Paso, the one in Scottsdale was at 5:00 a.m. The service with the marine honor guard was attended by numerous friends and relatives. Everybody cried as these proud marines honored one of their own with a twenty-one-gun salute, the playing of "Taps," and the flag presentation to Ms. Howard. I was honored to be asked to attend this service, and I really would have loved to have personally known this fine man and his wife.

After the service, I went to a reception that was being held. I knew very few people but felt as if I knew everyone. Ms. Howard introduced me to many people who thanked me for being there and for what I had done. I told them that although Robert and Cheryl were not with us, justice had finally prevailed because of the dedication of federal and local authorities, and I was just a small part of it. I met Cheryl's parents for the first time and received a handwritten card from her mother thanking me for all I had done. Again, I just said that I was a small part of this much larger investigation and that it was not over as the men who had committed the crime still had their day in court and needed to be prosecuted. To this day, I thank God they were.

As I began to write this story, I mentioned all the emotional strains that FBI SAs go through. I can honestly say that this was one case where I went from the highest of highs to the lowest of lows. I was elated whenever leads seemed to pan out and dejected when they were met with negative results. I worried that this young couple would never be found and rejoiced when they were. But then I wondered why I was rejoicing because they had been murdered. I wept with the mothers and also laughed with them as they related happier times. I questioned my own abilities to work this case when things went wrong and I could not bring Ms. Howard good news.

But, overall, recognizing the complexity of this case, I can honestly say that if I had to do it all over again, I would take this case on again in a heartbeat. It was such an emotional rollercoaster that I think of it quite often even though it happened over thirty years ago, and I still get a tear in my eye.

———◆———

I received a telephone call from a sergeant in the Phoenix Police Department. He said he was getting ready to leave headquarters to proceed to north Phoenix, where a small two-year-old boy had been kidnapped. A lady had been driving her car with her small son in the parking lot of a shopping center when someone confronted her at gunpoint and forced her and her two daughters out of the car. A young female jumped into the passenger seat, a young male jumped into the driver's seat, and they drove away, probably not realizing that this lady's young son was strapped into a car seat in the back. Police were called, and an APB was put out on this car and the young boy who was kidnapped. It was toward the end of the day, and traffic was atrocious. The parking lot was adjacent to a major freeway in Phoenix, and the car was driven away in an unknown direction.

All SAs were advised to proceed to this area to assist in working the kidnapping. Our SAs paired up with detectives and combed the area, trying to locate witnesses who might have seen something, but nothing could be established. One witness, a security guard, noted that a young couple had parked a van in the parking lot of a business complex, and when he confronted them about parking there, they pulled a gun out and ran off to the shopping-center parking lot. He called the police, and as he was doing this, the hijacking of the car was occurring almost simultaneously. It was determined that this van had been stolen the day before from a nearby auto dealership.

A search was conducted on this stolen van, and that led to some personal items that were recovered and related to a male named Dennis Mills and a female named Jennifer Day. This included address books and photographs of Mills and Day. Efforts to locate this couple were fruitless, and they became the prime suspects in this abduction. Of course, of paramount importance were the safety and recovery of this young child.

The search for the car went through the night, but it was not located. We were hoping the couple would drop the young boy off somewhere and see that he was returned to his mother. In fact, a news broadcast was put out to this effect, but there was no response from the kidnappers.

The following day, a Friday, a group of SAs started going through the many names and telephone numbers that we found in the van and made phone calls to these people. Many people knew the names of the young couple but said they had not seen them for quite a while. These calls were placed all over the country where the friends and associates were located. No one could shed any light as to where this young couple could have gone, but all agreed to call authorities if they heard from them.

An FBI official placed a telephone call to the nationally televised *America's Most Wanted* program that was being broadcast that Friday evening. We were made aware that if the FBI sent someone to Washington for the broadcast, they would put this ongoing investigation on their show. An SA provided the people at *America's Most Wanted* with the specifics of the case as I went home, grabbed a suitcase, and headed to the airport. The entire FBI office, in cooperation with the PXPD, was working this case to find the little boy. A detective from the PXPD was going with me to assist me on the program, so we met at the airport. Tickets were waiting for us for a flight to Washington with one stop in Dallas.

As the plane took off, I learned from the detective that this was the first time he had ever flown in an airplane, and he was really happy to go but was a bit nervous. We discussed what we needed to do to solve this case and have the boy returned home to his parents. We realized that this was now in the hands of God and the investigators on the ground, and there was not much we could do while flying to Washington.

Arriving in Dallas, I called the Phoenix office to see if there were any updates in the investigation and learned that the car had been spotted in Utah, and a chase was currently underway to stop whoever was in the car. Our continuation flight was getting ready to depart out of Dallas, so I was told to keep going on to Washington as they did not know if the child was in the car with whoever was running from the police. Needless to say, we were on pins and needles while flying to Washington.

Upon our arrival, I immediately called the Phoenix division to get the update. I learned that the chase had resulted in the car crashing into the side of the road with no injuries. The child was recovered unharmed, and the couple was arrested near Richfield, Utah.

The favorable results in locating this vehicle were due to the persistence of one of our young, aggressive first-office SAs. He was making telephone calls to friends of the couple whose names appeared in one of the address books. A person who was called said that he had not heard from them but would call the FBI if they contacted him.

It was about five minutes after this call was ended that the guy called this SA back and told him that right after they hung, he received a call from the couple saying they were coming up north to visit and asked if he could send them some money. He asked them where they were and told them he could send some money to help them. He then told them to go to the Western Union in the town they were calling from, and he would wire them some money. Immediately afterward, he called the SA and provided him with the specifics as to where the couple had called. He was directed to wire the money as agreed, and we would make sure he was reimbursed.

The SA had told the supervisor, and a telephone call was placed to the sheriff's office near where the young couple had called from. A deputy was dispatched to the Western Union and found the car as it was driving away. He gave chase, and the couple in the car sped away, traveling over one hundred miles an hour trying to escape. Eventually, they were caught and arrested; the young boy was recovered and thankfully was not injured.

The FBI sent a private airplane from Phoenix up to this area to return the child home to his parents, and they were reunited with each other that same evening.

Our office called *America's Most Wanted* and told them the child had been rescued and the couple arrested. It was not necessary to air this kidnapping on the program that evening. However, the detective and I were both invited to come to the television studio and watch the program as it was being televised and to work the phones if we desired to do so. So off we went and had a great time meeting the people who worked there, and we assisted by answering telephones and receiving information on the cases that were aired that evening. When we left, we were given

America's Most Wanted hats, and I got one for the young man who had been kidnapped back in Phoenix.

The next day, as we returned to Phoenix, the detective said he was enjoying the flight. I started messing with his head, and when there were a few bumps during the flight, I mentioned that they needed to put a bit more air in the tires. He just looked at me. I then pointed to the right wing and told him that the blinking light on the end was a turn indicator, and we would shortly be turning right. Again he just looked at me. Then as we passed over an obvious oval race track located far below, I told him to look down at it. I said it was a runway at a small airport for planes making round-trip returns. Now he knew that I was messing with him, but after we had returned to Phoenix, he relayed all these things to his friends at the PD, who tried to convince him that what I said was correct. We finally told him we were just messing around. What a great guy he was, and it was a real pleasure going with him on this trip to Washington.

In Phoenix, I went to the house where the parents and the young boy lived. There were television cameras still around, but by then the majority of events had been broadcast. I went to the door and was met by the parents. I told them I was the SA to whom the case was assigned. They were just great and very appreciative of what had been done to find their son. I gave them the hat for the young man, who seemed to be taking everything in stride. I spoke with him and learned that he had already received several football items from the Arizona Cardinals and was elated with these gifts. Mike Bidwell, a former AUSA with whom I had worked on several bank robbery cases and became friends with, is the son of the Cardinals owner and later took over as president and general counsel for the team. He graciously saw to it that this young man was recognized by the Cardinals for his bravery during this incident. Mike usually stayed in the background, and much of what he did went unnoticed, so this is just an opportunity to let others know what a class act he is.

After their arrest, Dennis Mills and Jennifer Day later entered guilty pleas to a number of charges ranging from assault charges to kidnapping and were sentenced to seventeen years' and sixteen years' prison time respectively.

CHAPTER 4

Crisis Negotiations

———

MIDWAY THROUGH MY CAREER, I became very interested in a program that the FBI Academy was offering to SAs in the field. Hostage and crisis negotiations were seen as valuable assets in the resolution of violent incidents that were occurring nationwide. Such incidents could range from a terrorist or a criminal holding hostages to seek a given demand, to a lost soul contemplating suicide. The basic principle was the same, and that was to find a resolution to the problem or incident without anyone being injured or killed. This sounds easier in principle than it is in reality. Trying to talk with a person who is emotionally involved in any crisis is exceptionally difficult. Our instructors at the FBI Academy in Quantico, Virginia, were selected because of their desire to establish the best negotiation school in the entire world, and, in my estimation, they accomplished their goal. They formulated lesson plans dealing with the hardest ingrained criminals to people who felt they had no more reason to live. Also, we were instructed on how to speak with people having mental issues and were given guidelines on how to deal with these various personalities. Speaking with someone who is extremely paranoid is much different from talking with someone who is determined to be a sociopath. Words make a difference.

Once we attended this course, we were expected to research all incidents found on our own, even if we were not involved in the incident.

If a crises negotiator with the Phoenix Police Department participated in a negotiation, it was my responsibility to learn all I could about the event and provide this information to the FBI Academy, especially if an unusual turn of events happened. We were all learning, and the more we became involved, the better we became.

Many of us became police instructors and taught crisis-negotiation topics and techniques to local and state agencies to educate them on the advancements made in this field. As a result, I was fortunate to meet and become acquainted with many great law-enforcement personnel in Arizona and, in fact, go to many of their crises incidents. Because of federal legislation, I could not negotiate if the incident was not a federal crime as I was a federal officer. I could, however, act as a consultant and offer advice to the negotiators if they needed any assistance. I must admit I probably learned more from them than they ever did from me. They engaged in many more incidents than I could ever dream of, but these incidents resulted in meeting and making professional relationships along the way.

I occasionally trained with our SWAT team in the Phoenix division, a great group of professionals dedicated to reacting and responding to the most dangerous events. I needed to know what they expected of me as a negotiator, and they needed to know what I could do to help them by gaining intelligence for them in the event they needed to make a dynamic entry to resolve a situation. They also needed to know what I expected from them. It was a two-way street, and if everyone cooperated, the results were often positive.

On one particular Saturday, the SWAT team was giving a demonstration to the entire office for anyone who wanted to see how the team performed in a dynamic entry. I was asked by SA Roger Browning, the SWAT team leader, if I would perform with them. He explained that they had constructed a small framed room with no walls so everyone could see inside the room. The demonstration tactic was to set up targets in the room, and the team would make the dynamic entry, throwing in a flash bang, a small exploding device that would cause a distraction to the criminals in the room. The team would then enter the room with live fire, shooting at the targets with live ammunition. Roger asked if I was interested in being the hostage sitting in the room as the SWAT team made entry. I had the utmost trust in our SWAT team and agreed to do this. Of course, we practiced all aspects of this entry so we could perform it in front of the audience. I knew that bullets would be flying past me during the exercise, and all I had to ensure was that I sat still and not move a muscle. What a great idea that was!

The day arrived for the demonstration. I wore a bullet-proof vest under a large shirt and sat on a chair in the middle of this room. Adjacent to and behind me over my right shoulder was a cardboard target representing one of the hostage takers. Two similar targets were placed to the left and right side of the room, representing other hostage takers. The audience gathered to watch at a safe distance, and it was explained to them that I was representing a hostage and that the SWAT team was going to rescue me with a dynamic entry. Just as everything was ready to go, it dawned on me that I had failed to put earplugs in, and I now realized this was going to get terribly loud, but calling a timeout was out of the question. The training exercise had already started. A large device exploded outside the room so as to create a diversion for the hostage takers who would have been in the room with me. Then, all of a sudden, the door attached to the framed room was blown open, and the flash bang was tossed inside and detonated, causing a ringing in my ears. I just sat there not moving and looked forward as I saw the SWAT team enter the room, shooting the targets with live ammo. I could hear the bullets hitting the head of the target over my right shoulder and then was thrown down to the ground by a member of the SWAT team, who covered me and made sure I did not move and was protected from any harm. It was over in a matter of seconds, but my ears were still ringing. It would take a period of time before they stopped.

After the demonstration, the audience was allowed to come forward to see the targets that the SWAT team had shot. They were amazed at the proficiency and professionalism of this team. One of the female support personnel approached me and told me that my right ear was bleeding. Apparently, my ear had been scratched when I was thrown to the ground by the SWAT team member, but I never felt a thing. I asked her if it was bleeding badly, and she said that it wasn't and just appeared to be scratched. She asked me what happened. I told her that Scott, a member of the team, had earlier asked me if he could shoot the tip of my ear off for realism, and I had given him permission. Her eyes widened as she believed he actually shot me. I then asked her if he shot much of my ear off, and she said the entire ear was still there but just bleeding somewhat. I said that was not a problem as long as he did not shoot my whole ear off. I let her believe this for a short time until others came up to see the ear that Scott shot. I then decided the joke might go too far, so I told everyone that I got the scratch on the ground and Scott did not shoot at my ear.

As I mentioned, I had complete trust in this group. I did not worry one bit that I would get shot by any one of them, but I always made sure that I kept them on my good side in the event that we were ever to do this again.

FBI swat team in live fire demonstration

Author "rescued" by swat team in live fire demonstration

Author with FBI swat team

One Friday, I was working a bank robbery in the far northwest part of Phoenix when the FBI dispatcher called and told me to immediately proceed to a bank located in the southern part of Scottsdale. Someone in the bank was holding over twenty hostages and was threatening to kill them. The Scottsdale Police Department (SPD) had already responded and had the perimeter of the bank secured. I had about an hour's drive to where I had to go since it was late afternoon on a Friday and traffic was unbearable. I advised the other agents at this bank robbery that I was going to Scottsdale, and they advised that they would also be responding as soon as they finished completing the work on this robbery in northwest Phoenix.

I left and proceeded to Scottsdale, and, as mentioned, the traffic was terrible. When the traffic is that bad, there is no sense using a red light and siren as all that does is stop traffic that you must maneuver to get around. I arrived at this bank as soon as I could and was directed to a house about a block away, where other negotiators from the Scottsdale PD were located. They established a site just adjacent to a command post where supervisors and all those in charge were located and could be contacted as needed.

Entering this residence, I was met by a great group of hostage negotiators from the SPD whom I knew personally through previous negotiation incidents or negotiation classes I had taught. They tried to start a conversation with the hostage taker, who refused to speak with them, telling them he wanted to deal with the FBI and not the SPD. So one of these negotiators looked at me, smiled, and said, "He's all yours." They briefed me as to what had transpired since they had arrived and made the initial telephonic communication with the bank.

A lone white male had entered the bank, announced this was a bank robbery as he pulled out a gun, told a teller to put the money in the bag he brought, and yelled for everyone in the bank to get down on the floor. Everyone complied, and they were very shaken by this man's demands. This subject then told someone to call the police and say the bank was being robbed and that he was holding everyone hostage. One of the bank employees did this, and the Scottsdale police responded, set up a perimeter around the bank, and shut down local streets, including Scottsdale Road, the main street leading into downtown Scottsdale.

The action of this robber was very unusual, and what immediately occurred to all of us is that this person wanted a confrontation with police. That was evident, but the question was why. The negotiators had no explanation because this person would not talk to anyone. They occasionally had an open line to the bank on the telephone and could hear him yelling and screaming, and he sounded extremely volatile. They had no idea who this person was. The SPD had officers looking at surrounding vehicles in nearby parking lots for any that might be apparent as belonging to this robber. So far, there was no luck in finding out because all the parking lots in adjacent shopping centers had hundreds of cars belonging to people who could be shopping. Nevertheless, they were trying.

I got on the phone and called the bank. A female teller whom I will call Linda answered with a shaken voice. I told Linda who I was and asked her to tell the robber who was demanding to talk to the FBI to come to the phone and speak with me.

Linda would be vital to the resolution of this matter because of her subsequent ability to remain calm in such a dangerous environment. She asked the person to come to the phone, and I could hear him yelling that he did not want to talk to me. He said that she would be an intermediary, verbally relay what I said to her, and provide me with his responses. I did not like this one bit as I wanted him on the line so I could get a better feel for what he demanded and perhaps pick up some inflection in his voice that could assist us. Although I could hear his response to Linda, it was not the same. I tried over and over to have her convince him to come to the phone, and all he did was tell her to hang up.

One trait of someone not wanting to talk with authorities is that the person might have a psychologically termed inadequate personality. He might be afraid that if I were to speak with him, I might convince him to release everyone in the bank and then surrender, and he did not want this to happen. I talked this over with the other negotiators who were monitoring our conversations, and they all agreed with this assessment. I solicited ideas from these other negotiators as to how to approach this, and we all threw some out, accepting some and rejecting others. But we all came to the conclusion that this person wanted this confrontation with authorities and was extremely dangerous and that talking him out of the bank without creating any violence would be extremely difficult.

While we were at this negotiation post, the FBI SWAT team gathered at the rear parking lot to enter the bank through a back door in the event it became necessary. It would have to be a dynamic entry since sneaking into the bank was out of the question because of its configuration. In other words, the team would toss in a flash bang to explode, causing disorientation of those in the bank by noise and flash and allowing the team to enter and temporarily neutralize the person holding the hostages.

Also, we had two FBI snipers positioned on a roof across the street from the bank, and they had an unobstructed view of the front door as they peered through their scopes. There was a tree in their line of sight that prevented them from viewing the entire interior of the bank, but they were positioned so they could take a shot if a decision was made to take this type of action. They could see through a portion of the bank window and view the subject inside, providing valuable intelligence as to his location and what everyone was doing. The one main drawback was that it was about 115 degrees outside (in case you didn't know, it gets scorching in Arizona in the summertime) and even hotter lying on top of this roof. One of the snipers would get in sight position and hold it for about ten minutes and then hand off to the second sniper, who would get in position so the first one could wipe the sweat from his dripping forehead. This went on for several hours.

One of the other difficulties we encountered was that the hostage taker had a shotgun. He tied the barrel of this weapon to the neck of one of the hostages and warned us that if we tried to enter, he would pull the trigger, and the hostage would die. We had to be extremely careful and even told him we did not want any accidents to occur. He just told us to do what he demanded and no one would get hurt.

We never referred to those being held as hostages as we wanted to personalize them with him. We referred to them as people just wanting to get home to their families and their children, always using language that made them appear to be ordinary people who just happened to be in the wrong place at the wrong time. This tactic seemed to have an effect on him as after a short time, he stopped calling them hostages and referred to each as a woman, a man, and so on.

Once we started negotiations again, he demanded a car so that he could make an escape from the bank. He would take several of the hostages with him, and once he was away, he would release them and leave. But if he was followed by the police, he would kill the hostages. We could not allow this to happen. We would not let him get away from the contained perimeter. We also realized that he was venting extreme anger as time progressed. He demanded that Scottsdale Road be opened to traffic, and we told him that would not happen. We explained that some citizen upset with him could breach the perimeter and come to the bank to harm him. He persisted a bit but eventually dropped this demand, never bringing it up again.

Linda later told me she went to the restroom, said a prayer, and asked God to take care of her children and husband as she believed she was going to die that day. This robber was so angry about all the occurring events that she was certain he was going to kill all of them.

I continued suggesting to him through Linda that surrender was his best option. We would work with him to resolve this issue since he had not hurt anyone, and this would work to his benefit. Perhaps he just needed a personal problem to get resolved, and we could put him in touch with those who might be able to help him. But the choice was his. He merely rejected all these pleas from us. We had doubted he would accept our offers, but we had offered them nevertheless.

Through all these demands and rejections over time, we asked him several times to release some of these people, and he subsequently agreed he would do so, releasing all but three of them. We advised the officers protecting the perimeter and those in charge that a release would happen, and when we told the hostages to start leaving the bank, they all came out the front and were met by police officers and SAs to be taken to safety. Those who were able were interviewed at this time to gain more intelligence for us.

Now we had three hostages in the bank: the hostage with the gun strapped to her neck, Linda, and one other female employee who refused to come out because she wanted to remain there with her two friends. This last employee remaining made it much harder for us because now we had three people to rescue instead of two.

Once we had all the hostages who exited the bank secured and out of danger, the robber started making demands again and now became furious with us for not allowing him to have a car to make an escape. We offered him the car but told him he could not take anyone with him. He rejected this, claiming that once he was outside, we would just shoot him. I told him that I would check again with my boss to get him a car. After I made several contacts with the command post, only to come back and tell him that he could not take any hostages with him, he became extremely upset and expressed more violence. He was screaming, and Linda said she believed he was going to shoot them. I told her just to try to remain calm and tell him I would check again with my boss on his demand for the car and for the hostages to leave.

I asked our SAC to come over, and SAC Jim Ahearn, a great authoritative figure, asked me what I wanted. I told him that since this robber was becoming more and more violent with his threats since we would not let him leave with any hostage, it was the consensus of all the negotiators that if something was not done soon to alleviate this matter, he would probably start shooting and maybe kill one of the hostages. He could then negotiate for the lives of the other two hostages. The SAC thanked me for the input, and I heard him tell the SWAT leader to advise the snipers they had a green light to shoot if the robber came out shooting. It was a last-resort decision but one that might be necessary to save the lives of the remaining hostages.

I then called back into the bank and told Linda to tell him that we could not get him the car and to ask him what else we could do to resolve this matter. Linda did not want to tell him this as she was afraid of his reaction. However, she did tell him what we asked her to do, and after relaying this to him, Linda said he was going wild. We could hear him screaming and yelling, creating even more fear in the three hostages inside the bank.

At this time, he went over to the front door of the bank, dragging the hostage with the shotgun tied to her neck. He opened the door about five inches and shot outside with a handgun, striking the grill of a truck that was parked in front of the bank and causing the radiator to explode with a loud boom. Immediately after hearing this large noise, I heard a distinct rifle shot. It was our sniper shooting at him through the five-inch slot in the door that he opened, striking him at the bridge of his nose, killing him instantly. His hands opened up, and the teller he was dragging around just sat on the floor. The FBI SWAT team entered through the back door, throwing in the flash bang and running to all the hostages to help them and going to the subject to make sure he could not harm anyone. One

SA went to the hostage who had the shotgun tied to her neck and re-moved it from her. The SWAT team then secured the area and called out a code four, notifying everyone that everything was OK and the subject was neutralized.

This entire episode, from his taking the shot out the front door to the securing of the bank by the SWAT team, took less than twenty seconds—a remarkable time considering the strain all personnel and hostages were going through, but it was uneventful because of the professional training the tactical team had undergone. This was normal for them, if a con-trolled chaos can ever be considered normal.

All hostages needing attention were taken to the hospital for treat-ment. One of them had been struck with some bone shrapnel from the subject, but it was minor, and she was released immediately. I went over to the bank and talked with Linda. She just came over and gave me a big hug, crying as she did so. I told her everything was fine now and that it was over.

I later talked with the sniper who had taken the final shot, and he said that when they were given the green light, both snipers drew down on the bank area. They could see the subject in the bank but did not want to risk a deflected shot through the window. When the subject opened the door and started shooting, he recognized the opportunity, knew he had only a second to respond before the door closed, and took the shot. He then turned to the other sniper and asked him if he had also shot. When he said he hadn't, the first sniper said, "OK. I got him."

We conducted an investigation into the identity of the hostage taker and found him to be a loner who was always in trouble but nothing of great consequence. When we contacted his brother to make the death notification, his brother said that although this incident and the death of his brother bothered him, he was not surprised by what his brother had done.

We also tried to figure out why the robber had hated the SPD to the point that he wanted a confrontation with them and would not talk to their negotiators. We never did find out the reason and thought that it might have been some incident of which there was no report taken. We never did find any car that belonged to him and never did determine how he arrived at the bank. We presumed that someone dropped him off there and would not come forward to admit doing so for fear of being charged with some crime.

It was too bad that we had to take a life to save several lives, but sometimes that initiative has to be taken. We would prefer for all these incidents to be resolved without any violence, but the decisions we make are based on the demands and conditions made by those we are negotiating with. We are fortunate to have such professionals as our snipers, who follow instructions to the letter and are thoroughly trained to do what is expected of them.

The following Monday, the bank was closed as it was being cleaned and repainted to eliminate any signs of the violence that had occurred. On Tuesday morning, at the request of bank personnel, I went to there and talked to the tellers and anyone else who had experienced the events of the past Friday. The teller who'd had the shotgun tied to her neck was crying and, although happy to be alive and sitting here, wanted to know why we had put her life at risk by shooting the hostage taker. I explained to her that her life was in danger the moment the subject tied the shotgun to her and that, although we had opportunities to shoot him through the plate-glass window, the snipers felt the risk was too high to commit to a shot. Therefore, he waited until there was a better opportunity so as not to harm her. The sniper also knew that shooting him at the precise location that he was aiming at would cause his hands to open and not pull the trigger, and so he considered this to be his only option. I told her that I completely understood her position, and she was entitled to feel as she did, but our concern for her safety was paramount in our decision-making. She said she felt better and understood but still had questions in her mind. I understand that several weeks later she resigned from the bank as she could not get beyond what had happened to her.

About a year later, I received a telephone call from a hostage negotiator in Baltimore, Maryland. He was organizing an annual negotiation seminar for negotiators throughout the country to be held in Baltimore and wanted me to speak concerning the events of this bank robbery. He also asked if I could find out if Linda could come and give her personal observations as the hostage teller.

I contacted bank officials in Phoenix, and they gave permission for Linda to attend if she so desired. I contacted her, and she said that she was not sure if she could do this as she hated to talk in front of a large group of people. I told her there would not be too many people attending, and she agreed that she would speak. I was not sure how many would be attending and did not ask, but I knew there would be more than a few. I sort of told a little white lie but also felt that her discussing the matter with a room full of experienced police officers would be a huge benefit to all, including her.

On the week of the seminar, we put her on a flight to Baltimore, and she was picked up by a representative who then gave her several tours of the area, including one in Washington, DC. I flew into Baltimore the next day but did not see Linda then. The next day, the multiday seminar started, and, at breakfast, I saw Linda. I went over to her, and she looked at me as if she wanted to kill me. I asked her what was wrong, and she said that there were hundreds of officers there for the seminar and she was very nervous. In addition, our presentation would be the very last one because of the vast impact it would have on the attendees. I told her not to worry about it and enjoy the next couple of days. She smiled but was very anxious.

Shortly before our presentation on the last day of the seminar, I told her I would get up before the group and explain what had happened during this robbery and the subsequent events. I would then introduce her to let her tell everyone what she went through and the emotions she felt. She had known this was the plan well beforehand, and I helped her work on her presentation as she took notes to remind herself. We saw the audience from where we sat, and I pointed out a person seated in the front row wearing a dark shirt and told her just to talk to him as if he were the only person the room and tell her story to him. Her hands were shaking, but I knew she would do fine. Anyone having the composure to go through the robbery as she did would get through this presentation with flying colors.

When our time came for the presentation, I got up before this vast group of negotiators from all over the country and described the events of the day of the robbery. I explained what happened and why we took the action we did, answering a few questions from several audience members. I then introduced Linda, who came to center stage to the applause of all these men and women in the audience. She looked down at the man in the dark shirt and started her story. After a moment or two, she was talking to all of them like a pro. She not only spoke to the man in the dark shirt but looked around and talked to all of them. She became very comfortable in a matter of moments and did a fantastic job explaining what she had gone through, hardly referring to her notes. She mentioned the moment she went to the restroom to pray, and I looked at the audience and watched as many of these people wiped the tears from their eyes—as did I.

When she finished her presentation, she turned and started leaving the stage. She turned to look at me as the entire room broke into applause, and she walked off to a standing ovation. She had tears in her eyes, and she came over to me and said if I ever did that to her again, she would get even with me. I just smiled at her, told her what a grand job she had done, and had her look to the audience for confirmation. They were still standing and clapping. The moderator of the conference went to the microphone and thanked her again, drawing more applause.

This conference ended, and many of those in the audience came over to us to thank us for such an excellent presentation. There was no question that Linda was the draw of the day, and she was remembered by many who attended. She was the real hero.

It was in the mid-nineties when I was contacted by another SA, first name Vince, in the Phoenix division. He told me he was interested in becoming a hostage negotiator and wanted information about it. He was very interested in negotiation tactics, and I suggested that he attend the FBI hostage-negotiation school in Quantico and learn all he could. He subsequently did this. When he completed the school, he became acquainted with some negotiators with local agencies in the Phoenix area and attended many of the actual incidents they engaged in to learn from their vast experience. I was contacted by many of these local negotiators, who praised his attitude and the assistance he was able to provide whenever he was with them.

One day I was contacted by the FBI SWAT team, asking if I could accompany them to an arrest they were going to make. The subject of this case was going to be arrested at his residence following an investigation of his ownership and operation of a men's club engaging in female stripping and possible prostitution as well as other crimes. The SWAT team did not know what to expect from this person or how he might react and wanted the negotiator to make a telephone call to the residence to bring him out into the waiting arms of the SWAT team. Also, if things turned bad, the negotiator would be there to help negotiate a surrender.

I told the SWAT team leader that I would be happy to help them out, but I suggested that we allow Vince to make the call to the residence to give him some experience. I would be there with Vince to help if he needed any, but from what I knew about Vince, he was quite capable of handling this by himself.

The following morning, Vince and I arrived at a location near the residence. We noticed that the SWAT team was gearing up to surround the house, and a time was set for the call to be made into the residence. An earlier surveillance from the night before had determined that the subject of the arrest was at home, so a simple call could be made to him in his house. We had the telephone number and waited for the green light to make the call once the team was in place.

I looked over at the person giving me the thumbs-up and told Vince to make the call to the residence. Vince punched the telephone number into the phone, and I heard him say, "This is the FBI. Come out with your hands up, and you will not be harmed!" Vince listened for a minute and then said, "Oh, OK," and then hung up the phone. I looked at him in amazement and asked what was wrong. Eyes down, he calmly said, "Wrong number." I just broke out laughing.

The SWAT team leader looked over at us and asked what the holdup was. I just said, "The line was busy. Hold on," acting a bit irritated for being questioned about this. As I was interacting with the SWAT team leader, Vince again punched the number in, this time taking his time, and then asked, "This is the FBI. Is this Robert?". Vince then said, "Good. This is the FBI. I need you to come outside with your hands up, and you will not be harmed. A special agent will approach you, and you are to take orders from him. Do you understand?" Vince then told him to open the door and come outside. We notified the SWAT team that he was coming out, and they said the door was opening, and the subject was being placed under arrest. Another job well done without incident.

I then looked over at Vince and broke out laughing. I promised him I would never tell anyone about what had happened, and he thanked me as he was somewhat embarrassed. No problem. This incident would never pass through my lips. I then suggested that he call back the first person he had called to tell them he could now go back inside his house and put his arms down. He did not think this was funny. I kept my word and did not divulge this to anyone at the office—until Friday, September 29, 1995.

This was the day I retired from the FBI. Several years earlier, my wife and I had moved to a retirement community in Peoria, Arizona, and she had rented out one of the halls for the retirement party. That evening, as I entered this building, there were all my family members, many of my golfing friends from where I lived, and many colleagues I had worked with throughout the years, including current and retired SAs and support personnel, who are the backbone of the FBI. I was honored by a number of attending personnel from various police agencies and attorneys as well as federal judges with whom I worked over the years. It was a night to remember, and I was humbled beyond what words can express.

This party included several of these people putting on various skits related to me, and one, in particular, was very ingenious. Remember Vince? Well, he dressed up as a Catholic nun and proceed to tell stories about me when I attended Catholic grade and high school. Seeing a nun with a mustache walking around in a black habit scolding me was hilarious. People were laughing so hard that Vince himself had a hard time talking without laughing. It was a great time, and I appreciated what he did.

Then it was my turn to get up and give a small speech. I started by thanking everyone who was present, with special thanks to all my family. I then had to thank Vince for his incredible performance as a nun but said there was a story that had to be told so that I could get even with Vince. I then proceeded to tell about the wrong number that he had punched in, and there was a roar from the crowd. Vince just stood there in half of his habit (he had removed the head part but kept the dress on), laughing with the rest of us. I apologized to him, telling him that I had to break my promise and relate the story that only he and I knew. Now everyone knew. He appreciated the humor in it and accepted it.

After I left the FBI, Vince transferred to Quantico and became a valuable asset to the behavioral-science unit at the FBI Academy. I've always wondered if he ever told future hostage negotiators about the time he punched in a wrong number.

———◆———

I had been a hostage/crisis negotiator for several years when I received a telephone call from SA Fred Lanceley, a negotiator and an instructor at the FBI Academy. He said that a crisis-negotiation team was being established to assist the hostage-rescue team (HRT) in the event that a negotiator was necessary for a particular crisis. This team was to receive additional and advanced training in hostage and crisis matters that could be imperative to case resolution. The team would consist of a total of twenty-five members the first year and would be increased year by year if found to be necessary. He asked if I would be interested in being on this team, and I accepted on the spot. It would be intense and exciting, and I would be in a cast of some of the best crises negotiators in the world. What an opportunity.

Once the team was established, we joined up at the FBI Academy, met one another, and formed a bond that could never be broken. I honestly believe that these negotiators were the best the FBI had to offer, and I truly looked forward to our yearly week of advanced negotiation instruction. It would prove to be educational as well as informative and eye opening. But those selected were what made the team successful. We referred to this team as the critical-incident-negotiation team (CINT) and, once established, it traveled around the world working on critical matters.

One member was called up to travel up the Amazon River in a boat to meet with hostage takers and worked on that case for months on end. A sidelight on this was when he rented the watercraft, he could not use a credit card, so he paid cash and later tried to recover this expense through his voucher. This expense was disallowed as any boat was considered a recreational vehicle and could not be covered. FBI HQ had never had this issue before, and so this was a first. Eventually, with the intervention of Quantico, the SA was compensated for his outlay of cash for this rental.

Other members would travel to other places in the world where the HRT went in the event they were needed. We had CINT at Waco to negotiate the Branch Davidian issue with David Koresh to prison rioting at various federal prisons. Anywhere we were needed, we would be there at a moment's notice. We would receive a telephone call and be told to leave immediately and prepare for an unlimited amount of days to be gone and negotiate. It could be from one day to several months, and the cases you were working at your assigned office still needed to be investigated, so it was good to have someone working with you who could help out when you were gone.

Since we were now working with other countries so extensively, once a year a representative from Scotland Yard in London, England, would send someone to attend the FBI hostage-negotiation class and learn our tactics of negotiation. The Metropolitan Police at Scotland Yard extended the invitation to our team, so we could learn firsthand negotiations techniques about terrorism. This was a two-week class, and in around 1990, I was selected to attend.

This was my first time to London, and it was quite impressive. Upon arrival, I was picked up at the airport by a Scotland Yard representative who made sure that I was taken care of until class started on Monday morning. I arrived on a Saturday to try to get through the jet lag, but that is a story in itself. It was not easy, but I did manage to accomplish it.

On Monday morning, I rose early, dressed in suit and tie, and met my new colleagues for breakfast at the academy restaurant. Very formal was my first impression, but that is the way of the British. After breakfast, we went to the classroom, which looked like a very elaborate library. There were no desks to sit at, but rather we sat on soft plush chairs, one for each student. We attended class until noon, broke for lunch, and returned to class for the afternoon, breaking around 4:30 p.m. to be prepared for dinner at 5:00. We then were allowed to change to casual clothing but had to be back in class at 6:00 p.m. We worked a practical problem for several hours and then broke to go to a room of relaxation to review and critique the solution. We were allowed drinks at this time and critiqued the problem into the early-morning hours. All drinking members tossed in ten pounds into a pot, and someone would go and buy the liquor for us for the evenings. I was a beer drinker, but it was awfully hard to drink warm beer. They did get me some ice, but I graduated to drinking scotch. Then it was off to bed to start the next day again. And this was the way it went for the next two weeks: extremely busy but very informative—and undertaken on very little sleep.

We learned about some events that had happened in England that I only knew about through news reports and briefings at the FBI. Now there I was meeting those involved in the actual events. I met and listened to Inspector Trevor Locke, who had been involved in the takeover of the Iranian Embassy at number 16 Prince's Gate, London. He had been rescued when the elite Special Air Service (SAS) assaulted the embassy and was instrumental in the resolution of that case. Trevor was a true gentleman in every sense of the word. We learned about the Irish Republican Army and the resolutions of many other incidents. This was quite a class and one I will never forget.

One member of our class belonged to the elite Special Boat Service (SBS), and we became good friends. When the rest of us were getting up in the mornings preparing to go to class, he was out running and scaling the buildings of the academy just to keep in shape. We all admired him, and on the final day, he came up to me and gave me his special necktie of the SBS, something I still have to this day. I gave him an FBI memento, but that tie is something I will always cherish.

The final Thursday consisted of an all-day practical problem where hostage takers (HTs) would be holding hostages at a house outside of London. All the negotiators in our class would be doing the negotiating and trying to get the hostages released. We knew in the final analysis that an elite HRT would be assaulting the building and rescuing them so as to give the HRT practice, but we could assist by gaining intelligence for them and having some of the hostages released.

We were briefed on Wednesday night as to what would transpire and what we would need to do. So we all gathered around to talk about it, knowing fully well that there were things we were not being made aware of just to put additional pressure on all of us. That was to be expected.

But I brought up a suggestion. I said we should have a great time using all the techniques we had learned and throw in something extra. I suggested that we adopt one word that everyone had to include in our narratives as we negotiated. We could not just toss the word in the negotiations, but we had to use it to fit into the actual negotiation itself. The word we all agreed to was "hippopotamus." We all kicked in five pounds (about eight dollars), and the negotiator who used the best line would be declared the winner and collect it all. We had twenty negotiators, so everyone paid the five pounds for a total of one hundred pounds or about $160. We gave this money to our class counselor, who would make sure the winner got it.

The next day, we all went out to the site, and the exercise began promptly at 8:00 a.m. The negotiators sat in a room in a chair facing a plate-glass window with a second and third negotiator to either side of him. On the other side of this window was a group of administrators who would be watching and listening to the negotiations in progress. They could hear and see everything that was going on. They had a series of lights they controlled, and these lights faced the negotiators. If the negotiator was doing well in his conversations with the HTs, the green light was on. If the negotiator strayed to a verbal area that the administrators did not want, a red light came on, basically telling the negotiator to return to what he had been talking about before. If the HTs became irate at the negotiators, a red light would come on. In other words, we would be directed as to the direction of the negotiations, and this was a tactic to see how we would respond under pressure.

To get started, the first negotiator had been talking to the HTs through a megaphone as they did not have a telephone in the house. The HTs asked to get a telephone, and the negotiator said it would be easier to find a hippopotamus in the woods than a telephone. Great line, and only nineteen more negotiators to go. The class counselor marked it down as a great line. However, we were then able to secure a portable telephone and introduce it into the house, so we could communicate by phone.

Several others started negotiations but could not get the adopted word into the narrative. We were limited in the time we had to negotiate as we had twenty negotiators, and they wanted each negotiator to talk for a select period of time. A few got the word "hippopotamus" in, but they did not make much sense. Then one negotiator got his chance and got his word in by saying it was hard to deal with the HTs as their skin was as tough as a hippopotamus's. Another great line! Mark it down.

Later on, it was my time, and when I got on, the HT said that I must be the Yankee because of my accent. He said he had been waiting for me and asked where I lived. I told him Arizona, and he asked where that was. I said in the United States. He asked me if I was just a smart ass. He knew it was in the United States but wanted to know where, so I told him. He finally said he knew where it was at, and I think he was playing me along just to get at me by asking all the questions and making me answer. I tried and tried to negotiate with this person, who was oblivious to anything I had to say. I finally said, "You know, in our country, we have an old saying. You can take a hippopotamus to water, but you can't make him drink." An obvious play on words. This HT went ballistic with me and started yelling, wanting to know what all this BS was with the hippopotamus. Here came the red lights, and the room was in a roar from everyone laughing. Our class counselor was behind me laughing so hard he had to turn his face away from the window so he could not be seen by the commanders. I was the only one not laughing as I started thinking that maybe this was not such a good idea. I could just see the powers that be at Scotland Yard filing a protest with the FBI for my making such light of a serious situation.

My time ended, another negotiator took over, and the negotiations continued. We had about another hour to go when one of the commanders running this operation came into the room where all of us negotiators were sitting and listening to the negotiations. He asked for three volunteers to take the place of the hostages. He pointed at me and said I was volunteer number one as the Yankee was always a volunteer. He then got two other volunteers and took all of us to the house where the HTs were holding the hostages. They allowed the female hostages to leave, and we were replacing them. The reason they were doing this was that the HRT would be assaulting the house with live ammunition, and we would be handled roughly and tossed about like rag dolls. It was easier to do with men than women. I now met the person I had been negotiating with, and he asked me on the side why everyone was using the word "hippopotamus," so I told him what we had done. He just started laughing, and he said it was working as they were getting tired of hearing us and would probably have surrendered just to shut us up. But we now had to go through the assault phase.

We were placed at various locations in the building away from each other and told just to sit down and wait. The rescue team would throw in flash bangs, and then the team would enter, firing live ammunition on the first floor. We were on the second floor and would be approached by the team after entry was made. They would take us outside until they could identify everyone, and then the exercise would conclude.

Sure as shooting, pun intended, the team made entry, the flash bangs blew, and the firing of the weapons started. I could hear the bullets striking objects on the first floor. I just sat there not moving a muscle. Then I was approached and turned over face first on the floor to be handcuffed. I was then handed parallel to the floor from man to man down the steps and carried outside. What a ride that was. I was put on the ground and told not to look up, and I did not as I could hear the sound of a ferocious dog near my head. Then several moments later, someone came forth and announced that the exercise was over, and it was a success. I looked up, and, sure enough, there was a dog about three feet from me looking mighty hungry. But he was with a handler, so I felt pretty safe. Nevertheless, I did not move until someone came over and helped me get up.

We went to a room where a quick critique of the incident was starting by all the commanders. Good points were discussed, and bad points were also mentioned. All of this was done so that when a real incident occurred, these fine men and women would be able to be fully prepared to do what they did best: rescue the victims and stabilize the situation.

I was anxious about our adopted word "hippopotamus" being used, but after the critique, one of the commanders brought it up. He said that was one of the best ideas ever as it made the negotiators think on their feet, livened up some tense moments, and made the event enjoyable. Our class counselor pointed at me and said it was the Yank's idea, and they thanked me. I just nodded like it was not a big deal. Thank God I would not have to go back to Phoenix and submit reports to FBI HQ explaining how I damaged relations with Scotland Yard.

It was getting late, and we were allowed to go to the nearby shower room to clean up and get ready for a formal dinner. We had brought our suits with us that morning as we knew we would be there all day and into the late evening. We got ready up and went to a very nice section where there was a bar next to the room where we would be dining. We bought several drinks and talked about the day and how great it had gone. We voted the best line for the adopted word, and I was declared the winner. I think they were just being nice as I believe the other lines by other negotiators were better. But I just took the money, gave it to the bartender, and told him to use it up for drinks for everyone until it was gone. I then gave him an extra twenty for a tip, and he said that since he was an employee, he would not take tips and would apply the extra twenty toward more drinks if I wanted.

We then went to the room for the formal dinner. Our lead instructor raised his glass and, on behalf of the Queen, toasted and thanked all who had attended the class and wished us all success. I rose and raised my glass and said that, as a representative of the United States of America and on behalf the president, I thanked the Queen, Great Britain, and Scotland Yard for this fine instruction. Everyone raised their glasses, saying, "Hear, hear!"

For a moment I felt important and then realized I was the one who had benefited from meeting such a great group of men who daily performed the same duties I did back in the United States.

I have maintained relations with some of these men and one in particular. Now-retired Inspector Dwight Atkinson and his wife, Lizzie, still correspond with me on a daily basis, and we have exchanged Christmas cards yearly, bringing everyone up to date on events in our personal lives. When I've visited London, Dwight has arranged special tours for me, including taking a photo of me standing in front of 10 Downing Street and touring the Thames River at night on a police launch. But the best times were standing with Dwight on the streets outside a pub and enjoying a pint with him. I also learned that ale was cool and not warm.

Author at Scotland Yard, London, England

CHAPTER 5

Confidential Sources

———————

MANY CASES INVESTIGATED BY LAW-ENFORCEMENT agencies are solved by utilizing the services of criminal informants (CIs). These are individuals who may obtain information from the criminal element about various crimes and then provide this information to someone in law enforcement. They do this for many reasons including rewards, continuing payments by the law-enforcement agency, revenge, and sometimes simply because they have consciences and want to see the guilty punished.

All SAs are required to cultivate these assets to use in gaining hands up on the criminal element and perhaps solving cases. This is not as easy as it sounds, and finding and cultivating an asset takes perseverance, patience, and luck. During our careers, SAs are always intertwined with individuals who either commit crimes or know someone who does. When a crime occurs, we will naturally interview all of our witnesses and then go into the trenches and alleyways to seek and find those who committed the crime. Therefore, when a suspect is developed, in many cases associates of theirs will be contacted to obtain additional information that could implicate the suspect in the case. In many cases, their associates will just tell us to go to hell. But nothing ventured, nothing gained.

Then there are those who provide information that may assist to such a degree that the case may be solved. For this reason alone, this information is extremely valuable and could result in either solving the case or letting it remain open as unsolved. Solving the case sooner rather than later results in the obvious: cost savings that allow the investigators to investigate additional cases, bringing justice to many more crime victims.

We were always on the lookout for those individuals who might provide this valuable information. The SA would try to form a bond with those people, and if the SA believed they might be helpful as CIs, the SA would open a case up for a time to evaluate the CIs and the information that they provided. Their identities would be protected, and they would be referred to by numbers and not by their names.

If the provided information resulted positively, the informant might be given a stipend for his or her efforts. The bigger the case that was solved, the bigger the pay. So this could be a great benefit to all SAs as the incentive to provide additional information was enhanced. Some informants could be paid monthly, and some would be paid as each case was solved. Obviously, the provided information had to be correct and corroborated to give the source any credibility.

But as mentioned, it is not that easy. As you might suspect, many of these people have engaged in criminal activity themselves, and that is how they came to be acquainted with these other felons. The SA has to ensure that the CI will not engage in criminal activity any further or do anything illegal to get any information being sought. In other words, it's like trying to get a zebra to change the color of its stripes. However, sometimes it works—and sometimes it doesn't.

—————◆—————

One source I opened to evaluate was a fun-loving guy who had just gotten out of jail after being convicted and serving prison time on a burglary charge. I met him during a bank robbery I was working and contacted him to ascertain if he knew a particular person who could have been involved in the crime. Unfortunately, he was not aware of the person, but as we talked over coffee in a restaurant, we developed a pretty good relationship with each other. When we finished talking, he told me that if he came across anything he believed might be of value, he would call me, and I could assess the information to see if it would help me. I gave him my phone number at the office and told him that he could reach me anytime, day or night.

Needless to say, our nighttime crew at the office even got tired of him calling looking for me, and after they patched him through to me at home on many occasions, I met up with him and had a talk with him. I told him that getting the license-plate number of someone running a red light was not what I wanted him to do. I was more interested in crimes of more substance. It took him a month or two, but he finally got the idea.

We met all the time, and he provided me with information that helped solve crimes of a local nature and not necessarily federal crimes. That was all right with me as I would take this information and provide it to local detectives in the town where the crime occurred, and this helped solve many crimes for them. I would seek a small payment for him for his assistance and would many times get the money for him. He was appreciative of this as he had a wife and small child, and this helped him provide for them.

One day, he contacted me and told me he needed to speak with me. I met him at a local restaurant, and he was very excited. He said he had developed some information about a fencing operation that was going on. Many burglaries were being committed, and the criminals were taking their stolen items to this business and could sell the stolen items for cash.

He believed this fencing operation was being operated either by the police or by the mafia because it was so elaborate. He gave me the address where the fencing operation was located, and I told him I would check it out and get back to him to see if he could gather any more information for me.

I returned to the office, immediately went to SA Ron Myers, and said, "Ron, I think my source is on to your fencing sting." I told Ron what my source had told me, gave him a photo of my CI, and said that I would thank my source for this information, asking for more details. Ron thanked me and told me he would keep me advised if he came across my source.

SA Myers was the coordinator of a sting fencing operation, working in conjunction with Phoenix detectives to purchase stolen property and identify those involved in the sales and burglaries. Once the sting program was terminated, the property would be returned to the victims of the burglaries, and those involved would be indicted, arrested, and tried for their crimes.

That afternoon, I contacted my source and told him I had checked, there were no police operations going on, and this must be a mafia operation. He said he would try to gather more information, and I told him that the FBI would look into it. He asked me if I was sure of what I was telling him. I looked at him like he was nuts and asked why he would question my integrity, and I reassured him that I was positive. He said he would try to get more information for me.

The next day, Ron came over to my desk and showed me a surveillance photo that had been taken at the sting fencing facility. Sure enough, there was my source with an armful of merchandise that he was selling. Ron had been able to get information as to where he had gotten the merchandise, and it was from a burglary that just occurred a week earlier. It was now obvious that my source was trying to find out from me if this was a police operation or not as he had this merchandise to fence and did not want to get arrested.

Ron said that his fencing sting was just about to conclude, and he was going to get warrants for everyone who had fenced anything. All the recovered merchandise through purchases needed to be returned to their rightful owners, so this operation would end in about a week or two. He asked me if I wanted to be on the arrest team that arrested my source, and I told him no but to just let me know when the arrest happened, and I would later go to the jail to pay him a visit.

I kept in contact with the source for the next week, and he kept asking me if I had determined if the people running the fencing operation were with the mafia. I just told him that I turned the information to our agents who work organized crime, and they would let me know when they found out for certain. However, they were very busy, and it might take several weeks or so before I knew.

About a week or so later, Ron told me that the arrests had been made, and my source had been arrested. I drafted a memo to the substantive CI file advising of this and closed this person out as a reliable source. He was a pretty good source, but after what he did, he could not be trusted and was now unreliable, and this was something that neither I nor the FBI would tolerate.

A week later, I went to a Maricopa County jail facility to interview a subject who was there. I checked records and found out that my source was incarcerated at this same facility. Once I was finished with my interview, I decided I would look him up to ask him about what had happened.

Needless to say, as I was walking to an interview room, there was my source delivering food trays to other inmates. I yelled out to him, and he saw me, waved to me, and came over. He was not very happy with me and told me that I was wrong in what I had told him about the fencing operation. He said it was a police operation, and he could not understand why I did not know that.

I asked him how dumb he thought I was. Did he believe that I would tell him about a confidential operation that was going on? He said that he did because we had this "special" trust with each other. Excuse me. Special trust?

I asked him why he was committing all these crimes by breaking into homes. Was he trying to find out if the fencing operation was a police sting? Was this so he would not go there to fence his merchandise and possibly be arrested? Of course he denied all this but could not escape the fact that he had been caught on tape fencing all of his stolen merchandise.

He asked me if I could get him out of jail so he could go back to work for me, and I said that would not happen. He needed to answer for his actions, and he could no longer do anything for me as now I did not find him to be reliable. We shook hands, and then he went his way, and I went mine.

About a year later, he called to tell me he had gotten out of jail and wanted to meet up with me. I met him at a restaurant. He ordered a hamburger, fries, and a Coke, and I had coffee. He apologized to me and said he had learned his lesson and wanted to start getting information for me again. I just looked at him, and it was obvious he was drugged up and looked like hell. I told him that would not happen again, and he said he was desperate, pointing out to the parking lot and his beat-up car. Inside were his wife and small child. He stated that they had not eaten for a day or so and were hungry, and he needed money for them to eat. I about lost it with him. Here he was eating a giant hamburger and fries, drinking soda, and obviously high on drugs, and he did not think to take any of the food to his family. I told him he needed help for his drug addiction, and he said he knew he did. He said he had been put on probation for all his burglaries and had a probation officer. I told him to try to get help through this officer because if he didn't, he would be dead in a year, and he was not doing his family any good. His eyes teared up, and although I felt sorry for him, I knew he had to do this for himself, and there was nothing else I could do for him.

I ordered several more hamburgers and fries with sodas to go, and when they came to the table, we both got up, I paid the bill, and we walked out to the car, where I gave the food to his family. He thanked me for that and then asked if I could give him some money. I just looked down at his wife, who was quiet but closed her teary eyes and shook her head. I told him that I could not provide him with money for drugs and that I would not give him any. He just shook his head, got into the car, and left as I went to my car.

I never saw him again.

———◆———

One day I was called by a robbery detective from the Phoenix PD who worked with an officer in another division at the PXPD named Robert. Robert talked with a person named Jimmy; he was serving a prison term and had some information to pass on to the FBI about a very important matter. I told him that I could meet with Jimmy to see what he wanted.

Robert and I went to the Maricopa County jail, where Jimmy was incarcerated. Jimmy said that he had talked to some friends who told him that the manager of a large bank in Phoenix was going to be kidnapped and held for ransom. Jimmy then stopped talking. I told him to continue, but he said he didn't know any more. However, if I could work with him to see that a long sentence he had just received could be reduced, he could probably find out more for me. However, to do this, he needed to get out of jail, and then he would be free to go out and develop the information for me. Jimmy also said that he knew that he was being a snitch, in police parlance, and had no problem with this as long as I did not identify him to anyone as the person providing the information.

I left the jail and talked with Robert, who said he believed what Jimmy had to say. Jimmy had apparently provided him with information in the past, and the information had been valid. I told Robert I had my doubts, but on the other hand, I certainly would not want to disregard the information and then have an extortion attempt take place. He agreed and said he also had some doubts but was willing to at least have Jimmy removed from jail to see what he could develop for us.

To keep Jimmy's name out of anything, I decided to open him up as a PCI (potential criminal informant). In the meantime, Robert did all the necessary legwork to see if he could remove Jimmy from jail to help us on this case and was able to get him released. We met up with Jimmy and in no uncertain terms told him that he was going to get the information for us, and if he hoped to use us just to get out of jail and then run off, he was dealing with the wrong people. I would go to extreme lengths to find him, arrest him, and then charge him with providing false information to a federal agent. He said he understood all this but knew that if he could get the information for us, he could prevent an extortion from happening.

He also knew this would possibly help him from serving a long sentence on his previous conviction. I told him to go out, see his friends, and see what he could find out.

Jimmy was out for several days and called and said he had identified the bank that was going to be targeted by the extortionists but nothing more. Then the next day, he said he believed he had the first name of who might be involved and was going to meet up with that person later that evening. I told him that I wanted him to come with his car to the FBI office in the late afternoon. It was my intent to have our own personnel install recording devices in the car and on Jimmy's person, so we could get all transmissions as well as recordings of all conversations. Also, we would put a surveillance team on him to see when and where he went and whom he saw in hopes of identifying the person who would be committing this extortion.

Jimmy never showed up at the appointed hour to have any of this done. He called me the following morning, was very apologetic, and said that he was with several of his friends and could not get away from them. In addition, he would not have been meeting up with the person he thought he would meet, so now it was just a matter of time before he could find that person to talk with him.

I told him to come to the FBI office as soon as he could as I wanted to talk with him. I then called Robert and told him what had happened, and he was not too happy with Jimmy. I asked Robert if he could set up a polygraph exam for Jimmy right away, and he told me to bring Jimmy down to the PXPD, and it would be set up.

As soon as Jimmy arrived, I told him he was going to take a polygraph test, and he had no problem with that. We went to the PXPD, and he was given the test by their examiner. The results were that Jimmy was responsive and was not deceptive in any of his answers. Was he telling the truth, or was this just a person with a very abnormal personality that would allow him to lie and make him appear to pass the polygraph exam? At this time, we had no way of knowing. Nevertheless, we worked with Jimmy again, and I told him to let me know when he would be meeting up with the extortionist.

Several days went by, and it was now about a week or so since he had been released from jail in efforts to gain more information for us. I was sitting at my desk when a bank-robbery alarm came in from a Scottsdale bank. Kelly, our radio dispatcher, contacted the bank to verify the robbery and gain whatever description she could from bank personnel, so she could broadcast this information to all responding FBI units. I started to leave to go to the robbery and was paged to call the radio room. Kelly told me she had been advised by bank personnel that the person who robbed the bank had told the victim teller to call Tony from the FBI and tell me that he had been forced to rob the bank and provide the teller with his name. Well, Jimmy did it; he robbed the bank. We put out an all-points bulletin (APB) to all FBI units and local agencies for Jimmy and the car he was driving.

As I was responding, Kelly radioed me and told me that Jimmy had called the FBI office and told us where he was parked. She notified all the units and also local agencies. A PXPD unit found his car parked where he said he would be and placed Jimmy in handcuffs while they waited for us to respond. I got there and met Robert and the robbery detective from the PXPD who was working with all of us on this original case.

Jimmy said that some individuals had told him that they knew he was snitching on them and then ordered him to rob the bank. After the robbery, they had followed him to this location and taken all the money from him and told him that if he snitched and told authorities who they were, they would kill him. We told him we had a hard time believing him and asked where the money was. He said they had taken it, and that is why he did not have it.

We had a marked PXPD unit transport Jimmy to the PXPD head-quarters. Robert set up another polygraph exam for him, and Jimmy agreed to take it. In the meantime, we searched his car and had it towed to police headquarters.

The robbery detective who was with us noticed during this search of the car that there happened to be some tumbleweed residue in one back wheel well of his vehicle. We surmised he would not have had this weed stuck in the wheel well unless he had driven out into the desert. He had earlier directed us to meet in a parking lot of a huge shopping center adjacent to the desert north of town, where he was found parked by the PXPD unit. Having this tumbleweed in the wheel well was unusual, and we wanted to see what he said about it.

We called Robert and told him to have the polygraph examiner ask him if he knew where the money was and if he had been out in the desert. We then departed for headquarters to find out the polygraph results and reinterview Jimmy.

Upon arriving there, we learned that Jimmy had again passed the polygraph exam with flying colors. We took him, put him into an inter-view room, and started questioning him again. He stayed with his story that he had been forced to rob the bank and give the money over to those who made him rob the bank. He reiterated that he had gone to that huge parking lot and given the money to them at that location.

Once we had this story, we asked him if there was anything else he wanted to add and if this was the exact story of what happened. He said he would not change a thing and that he had been completely honest with us.

The detective got up and just turned his back to Jimmy. He said he was getting very upset, and I told Jimmy that he did not want to upset this particular detective. We could help him down the line, but we did not like being deceived. Jimmy said he was not lying. The detective just turned around, slammed his hand on the table, and asked him how the tumbleweed got into his wheel well. Jimmy asked what tumbleweed we were talking about, and we told him about the one we had found and taken photos of. The film was being developed as we talked, and we would show them to him shortly. We could see that Jimmy was getting rattled, but before he could get a chance to think of an excuse, the detective said, "You were out in the desert, weren't you? You took the money and buried it out in the desert and then came to the parking lot where we met you. Don't lie. We know you were there. We know more than you think we know."

Jimmy just said, "You had the bird on me, didn't you?" He was referring to a surveillance aircraft that he knew we were going to use on the extortion allegation that he had earlier made. He must have believed that we were following him all along and saw him commit the robbery, take the money to the desert, and later meet up with us.

We just said that we knew more than Jimmy believed we knew, so now was the time to come clean and tell us the entire story. He then described the general vicinity of the desert where he had buried the money. We had some SAs go to that area, and after searching for a few minutes, they located and recovered the money taken from the bank. He then proceeded to give us a complete statement of the robbery and the fact that there was no one else involved. In addition, he said that the story of the extortion was bogus. He did not know of any extortion. I told him if one happened in the near future, he would be the first one I would suspect as being involved. He said that he had just used that as an excuse to get out of jail.

Jimmy was charged by local authorities with the bank robbery and was sentenced to a long prison term.

Some years later, I learned from the parole-and-probation office that Jimmy was going to be released from prison, and a date was provided. I notified all local agencies in the event a robbery of some sort happened, and he became a suspect.

Several months later, I was contacted by a homicide detective from the PXPD. He told me he had a homicide he was investigating and believed that the victim had been associating with a female who was dating a local biker. The victim had been told by this biker to leave her alone, and he'd refused, so someone had taken some violent action. This detective learned that the victim could be someone named Jimmy and asked me if I had photos of tattoos that Jimmy had. He knew the prison had them, but if I had them, he could find out quicker. I told him I did and met up with him. He looked at the photo and said that was the photo of a tattoo that was on the left leg of his victim. He said that was all he had—the left leg. Apparently, Jimmy was killed and dismembered. This leg was found in a trash bin. They were looking for other parts but never could find any more. Their source said that Jimmy was killed by unknown persons. The PXPD had many suspects but nothing that would convict them for this murder. No other body parts were ever found.

The question was often asked as to how Jimmy was able to pass the polygraph exam. In my opinion, Jimmy had an antisocial personality. He was very manipulative and cagey. He used his charm to gain what he wanted and was able to read people very well. As in past convictions, he had no remorse for any of his past deeds and claimed that he was changing his ways to do better in life. Such are the characteristics of an antisocial personality. Many people who possess this type of personality can readily pass these polygraph exams with ease.

CHAPTER 6

Miscellaneous Duties

———◆———

THERE ARE MANY STORIES THAT I can recount that do not fall into any one particular category but will present themselves occasionally during any given workday. Some may be just stories of other SAs that have a light tone to them, and others might be memorable in other ways. Some just stay with a person forever and are remembered because of the characters involved and just need to be told to be appreciated. Such are the following.

———◆———

One of my specialties as an SA was fingerprints. When I first hired on with the FBI, I worked in Washington, DC, at the identification division, where I evaluated fingerprint cards. I learned how to classify a fingerprint card and compare the prints on that card with the millions of fingerprint cards that were filed at the identification division. Working in the division for about four years helped me become an expert in fingerprint identification, which I found assisted me when I was an SA. I testified in federal court on many occasions, where I was certified as a fingerprint expert. When I worked fugitives, I was able to look at the fingerprints of a detained suspect and either identify that person or eliminate that person with 100 percent certainty as being the person we were seeking.

In addition, I was a fingerprint instructor for the FBI and taught numerous forty-hour fingerprint-classification courses to local police agencies, primarily in Arizona but in other states as well. I also taught latent-print techniques that allowed local police agencies to learn the various techniques in locating fingerprints at crime scenes by processing these hidden fingerprints with chemicals or dusting powder and preserving them for later identification and court testimony. This was a very valuable asset to me in my progress as an SA, but the problem was that I was constantly being called upon by other SAs to assist them whenever fingerprints became an issue.

Perhaps you have seen a fingerprint card. If not, here is a brief explanation. When a person is fingerprinted, the subject would be brought to the fingerprint room, and a small dab of a thick fingerprint ink is rolled out to a thin film on a smooth surface such as a layer of glass or metal plate. Once the ink is rolled out to this thin layer, the subject's fingers are rolled out individually, and this ink is transferred to the ridges of the finger. The finger is then rolled out on the fingerprint card in a specific order so that all the ridge detail of the finger is displayed on the card. (Today, many agencies have advanced fingerprint technology that will read and print the fingerprint automatically, and the finger does not need any ink application to be transferred to the card.)

This procedure is not very difficult with a little practice, but the problem is defined by the condition of the fingers. If the fingers have very small or fine ridge detail on the first joint of the fingers, it is very easy to use too much ink and smear the prints, making them unusable. Anyone who is an expert in fingerprints can readily tell if the prints are sufficient or insufficient for submission to the FBI for further processing. As a result, I was often called upon to assist other SAs who were not quite as familiar with fingerprints as I was.

———————

One day a young SA called me on the phone and asked if I could help him. He was investigating a case and needed fingerprints from one of his suspects. He contacted the AUSA who was working with him on this case and was able to secure a subpoena from a judge for the subject to appear at the FBI office and have his fingerprints taken. He wanted me to take the fingerprints. I agreed to help him and said to let me know when the suspect came to the office.

He shortly called and said that the suspect had arrived but that he had to talk to him for a short time and would be ready in about ten minutes or so. He would take the person to the fingerprint room at that time and wait for me.

At about this time, I received a telephone call on one of my cases and got wrapped up in the conversation. I was in another world, forgetting about going down to the fingerprint room, when another SA came over to my desk, laughing loudly, as he said I might go help out the SA in the fingerprint room, who was having a problem getting prints from his subject.

I immediately left my desk and went to the fingerprint room. When I got there, I saw this SA with his white shirtsleeves rolled up past his elbows with ink all over his hands and arms. He had black ink on his white shirt and ink on the walls. I looked at the suspect, who had a look of wonderment in his eyes with all the ink on his hands. He looked at me, and as he did, I just broke out laughing. The SA was cussing because of all the mess he had made. I apologized for being late but said I was busy on one of my cases. He said he was not mad at me but upset with all the ink that was all over the place.

I told the SA to wipe his hands off, take the subject to the restroom, and spray some fingerprint-ink remover from the can I handed him. While they were gone, I cleaned off the fingerprint equipment and reapplied fingerprint ink on the smooth plate glass and waited for the subject to return. Once he did, I took his fingerprints in about three minutes or so. He asked me why I did it so easily and why the other SA had made a mess. I just said that I was comfortable doing it and that he would learn in time. The SA was standing there and took the subject out to the elevator so he could leave. The subject was accompanied by a friend of his, and as I walked out toward the elevator to go to another location, he pointed at me and told his friend, "That's the guy who saved me." His friend said that he was getting ready to leave as he thought we must have arrested his friend as it took so long for him to come out.

After the subject and his friend left, I took the SA into the fingerprint room to show him the proper way to take fingerprints. I asked him what he did earlier, and he said that he just took the fingerprint tube and took the ink from the tube and put the ink on the suspect's fingers, much like taking a tube of toothpaste and putting the toothpaste on a toothbrush. Then he took the finger and rolled it on the card, but all he got was one big mess. I showed him where he was making his mistake, and now he understood how to take the prints.

Of course, he could not get all the ink off of the walls, and he tried and tried to clean the ink off, but it was impossible. He went to the support-personnel supervisor, told him what he had done, and offered to paint the walls to make them appear like they were before he put ink on them. This supervisor got him some paint and a brush and made him paint the wall. Good for both of them.

———————

In my first office in Columbia, South Carolina, I was assigned to work any criminal violations that occurred at the military base at Fort Jackson. Any crime from shoplifting to murder was assigned to me, and I was assisted by military investigators from the criminal investigative division (CID) and the provost marshal's office. These were extremely hardworking investigators and police officers whom I could always count on to help set up interviews and assist me whenever I needed additional help in any case. Needless to say, I always reciprocated whenever I could.

One Friday, one of the investigators called me and said that a body had been found on one of the rifle ranges, and they could not determine if foul play was involved or if the person had died of natural causes. I said that I was coming right out and would meet them at the main gate, so they could direct me to the range where this body was located.

Upon arrival, I followed the CID to the area where the body rested. The military police and CID had already roped off the area where the body was, and an ambulance for transport was available. There was no question that something was there as the stench of the decaying body was horrible. It was an incredibly hot day, and from initial appearance, it looked as if the body had been there for a week or two. The body was deteriorating with dark body fluids soaking into the ground and clothing on this person. The majority of the person's face had been eaten away by maggots and wild animals. It was difficult to ascertain the person's sex.

The CID investigator advised that a search of the surrounding area had not turned up anything unusual except for a few playing cards and a small plastic chair about three inches tall that appeared to be a child's toy. Except for the decaying condition of this body, there did not seem to be any evidence of violence.

I needed to determine that a crime had occurred so that the FBI could assume jurisdiction. I could still assist in identifying the person through fingerprints or other means. After discussing this with officials who were present, I suggested that medical personnel perform an autopsy in an effort so see if this person had expired through natural causes or been the victim of foul play.

Here was where everything turned around. For the FBI to assume jurisdiction, we had to show that this person was not military personnel and was the victim of a crime. For the military to assume jurisdiction, they had to show this person was from the military. No one here believed that this person was from the military. The body was clothed in a white jumpsuit that was heavily stained by the body fluids. Because of this fluid staining on the clothing, it was not only difficult but almost impossible to see if there was any writing on the jumpsuit. If there was a name or company logo on the clothing, it could not be seen.

The military medical personnel advised they could not perform an autopsy since there was no way to say this person was from the military. To have an autopsy performed, they advised that the Richland County Medical Examiners (ME) Office needed to conduct the autopsy. However, the problem was that the ME could not do the autopsy since the body had been found on a military base and not in Richland County. So now we needed an autopsy to be performed to determine if there had been any potential violence, and we could not get anyone to do the autopsy. I told them that if there were just a hint of violence, I would open up a murder case and work it accordingly. But I needed as least a semblance of violence to do this. I could not arbitrarily open a case just for the sake of it. I needed something to justify my decision.

We now had a standoff. I felt sorry for the poor ambulance drivers, who had been here all afternoon in the stifling heat. The medical personnel told me that I should direct these ambulances where I wanted the body transported as there was nothing more they could do, and they left the area. I looked over at the CID investigators, who were as quizzically amazed as I was. I was getting a bit upset as I was trying to do the best I could but never in a thousand years would be able to convince the Richland County ME to perform the autopsy. I had to make a decision on what to do with the body.

But what could I do? Being facetious, I told the other investigators I could not take the body home with me. Our office was out of the question. So after discussing this with the CID, we did what only we could do. We told the ambulance drivers that this body should be placed in the ambulance and driven to the hospital on base and that they should notify officials at the base hospital that they had the body and wanted to know what to do with it. It would have to be up to those officials to at least take the body in and do a cursory examination to see if any violence could be noted. If so, I could then assume the jurisdiction and would continue to see that someone perform the autopsy.

I told them to advise the medical personnel that when they came to a decision, they could call me, and I would return to help them out. I then left and returned to the office. I typed up a memo explaining what had happened and did not hear from anyone at Fort Jackson, so I went home.

At about 7:00 p.m., I received a telephone call from a doctor at the hospital who stated they were going to bring the body inside and have several doctors examine it, but they wanted me to be present. I said I would be there as soon as I could. Rather than going to the office to get an FBI car, I just drove straight out to the hospital at Fort Jackson in my personal car.

Upon arrival, I was directed to a room where the doctors were examining the body and was given a gas mask so that I would be able to breathe through the stench in the room. The body was face up on the table while doctors took x-rays and examined it, doing one extensive and professional examination. As they worked on the body, I looked at the clothing that was removed from the corpse. I noticed a small notation on the inside collar and pointed this out to a CID investigator who was also present. We tried to remove some of the dark body fluid from this area and, succeeding, determined it was a name of a state housing facility for the homeless and mentally ill.

As the doctors took x-rays of the body, they removed the x-ray plates that were near the top of the body and shook them off on the floor to rid them of the maggots that crawled on them. I looked down at my feet through the limited vision I had with the gas mask on and could see these invasive maggots crawling on my shoes.

Boy, did I do some dancing around! I said a few choice words, but the assistant helping the doctors wondered why I was so upset. He was accustomed to doing this all the time. I wasn't.

I then left the examination room and went into another room and obtained the telephone number of this state housing facility noted on the clothing of this deceased person. I called, identified myself, and asked to speak to the administrator and was put in touch with him. I explained what I was doing, and he said that many of the people living at this facility wore white jumpsuits. He asked me to describe this person, and I told him that would be difficult because of the condition of the body. I then suggested that from all appearances this person had been dead for at least a week or more. The administrator said he needed to check his records and put me on hold.

After a few moments, he advised that about ten days earlier a black male had walked away from the facility, and he had not returned. I asked him about the man's family and was told the person who left had no immediate family, and that was the reason he was living at this facility. He said that he knew just about all the residents at the facility, and this particular person was an elderly gentleman who was somewhat mentally impaired. I told him about the playing cards and small highchair we found, and he said the person he knew always had a little toy highchair with him, telling everyone it belonged to his grandchild. But the administrator said this person had no living family member and just said this so that everyone would believe he was not alone in this world.

I asked if he had a set of fingerprints for this person, and he said there was a fingerprint card in his patient file. I asked him for permission to use these to make an identification, and I would have an officer from the Richland County Sheriff's Office pick them up. I would return them when I completed the identification. He said he would make these prints available.

I returned to the examination room and told everyone that we might know who this person was. I told them I needed to get some fingerprints from this corpse, and the doctor said that he would handle it. He also stated that the cursory examination had provided no information that would indicate this person died because of foul play. It appeared this person might just have collapsed at the range and died of natural causes.

I contacted a friend from the Richland County Sheriff's Office fingerprint section, and he said that he would have a deputy pick up the prints for me at the housing facility. They would wait for me to come to the identification bureau and might be of assistance in making the identification.

I returned to the examination room, and the doctor handed me a sealed plastic bag containing formaldehyde and a severed right hand. This was not what I had in mind when I asked for fingerprints, and the doctor said this was done all the time, and he had authorized the removal of the right hand. I signed for taking this severed hand with me and told the doctors that I would call them when I made the identification of the deceased. They advised that once the identification was made, they would transport the body to the medical facility at the state, so arrangements could be made for burial.

So there I was leaving the base hospital with a small plastic bag containing a human hand. It was about 3:00 a.m., and as I drove down darkened streets, I could not help but think of the movie about a severed hand crawling up the back of a car seat. I kept my eyes on the plastic bag, which was lying on the passenger seat, and it seemed like a lifetime before I arrived at Richland County Sheriff's Office.

I entered this facility and had the deputy on duty take me to my friend who was waiting for me with the fingerprint card. I showed him the hand floating in the liquid in the sealed bag. He got me a fingerprint glass, and I was able to separate one finger in the bag and press it against the inside of the bag. I looked at the print and then the same finger on the fingerprint card obtained from the housing facility. There was no question that the prints were identical to one another. I had this verified by the person on duty, who said he would write a report on the identification, so it would be available if any questions surfaced.

I sat down and had a cup of coffee and talked about what had happened that day. At that time, another officer on duty happened to come into the room and see the plastic bag lying on the counter. The liquid in the bag was very dirty, and the hand could not easily be seen. The deputy thought it was a fish that someone had brought into the building, so he picked it up to look at the fish. Once he realized what he had, he dropped it and went ballistic. He told us he did not think it was a funny joke. We said it was no joke, and no one had asked him to pick it up, but he felt that we should have warned him, and he walked out of the room.

When I left the sheriff's office, I took the fingerprints and the sealed bag with me and drove to the housing facility. I was met at the gate by a security guard, and I told him who I was. He said he was expecting me and that the military was transporting one of the former residents, who was now deceased. I asked him what was going to happen to this man, and he said that since he had no family, he would be buried at Potters Field, a cemetery for those unfortunate few not having any family.

I gave him the fingerprint card and a paper bag containing the playing cards and small highchair that we recovered. Also, I gave him another paper bag containing the sealed plastic bag and severed hand and told him these were remains of this man. I asked that he take these remains and put them with the body that was being returned, and he said he would. He signed a receipt for all these items, and I left.

As I was leaving, he told me for what it was worth, I should go home and take a shower as it was pretty evident that a certain stench was hanging on me. I thanked him as he smiled and told him that I had already been told this by a couple of deputies from Richland County.

I got home at about 5:00 a.m. on this Saturday morning, went into the garage, and stripped down, putting all the clothes into a paper bag and that bag into another bag. I then took them out to the trash can and threw them away. Even the shoes. They all had a stench on them, but the memories of this case were going to linger with me as I thought of that poor elderly gentleman who had died over a week ago.

I then went into the house, showered, and went to bed. Rosie stirred as I got in bed, and I asked her if she would mind taking the car to get it washed both outside and inside, and she said she would later in the morning.

She did, and when I woke up, I heard all about it. But at least the stench would not linger for much longer.

———◆———

There was a time when I fingerprinted a potential FBI employee. This person applied to work for the FBI, and to conduct a complete background investigation on her, it was necessary to take her fingerprints, submit them to the FBI HQ identification division, and see if she had any previous arrest record.

I rolled out the ink on the glass plate, individually rolled out her fingers over this ink, and transferred the inked finger to the fingerprint card. Once done, I checked the card to make sure all the fingerprints were adequate for searching and, when that was done, told her that we could clean her hands and remove the ink from her fingers.

I took the can of spray and sprayed her fingers, and the ink became very liquid. She was amazed how quick this was working as the ink appeared to be just dripping off. I was also surprised as I had never seen this happen before. I took a paper towel and wiped her hands off, but the ink was still very evident, so I sprayed again, and the ink only got darker. I wiped her hands again and could not understand why this was happening. I looked at the can of spray and only then realized that someone had put a can of liquid ink spray near the can of the spray to remove the ink. What I had been doing was spraying liquid ink on her fingers, and it appeared the ink was being removed, but that was not the case. So I put it back and sprayed the other ink-remover spray on her fingers and was able to remove the ink. I did not tell her what had happened other than the other spray must have been defective. She never knew the difference.

After she left, I contacted the person who kept the room supplied with equipment, and he said that he had found this liquid ink on the market and thought it might help, so he bought it and placed it in the room. I told him this ink was liquid and too thin to be used, that it was not for fingerprinting, and that he should remove it and never put it back in the room again. I told him what had happened, and after laughing for a couple of minutes, he asked me why I sprayed her hands with this ink. I was the fingerprint expert and should have known the difference. Needless to say, everywhere I went that day, I was met by many others asking me if I had tried out the new fingerprint spray.

———

I had just been assigned to the bank-robbery squad in the Phoenix division and was falling in line pretty quickly. There was a number of newer SAs such as me as well as older veteran SAs on this squad. One veteran who will always be remembered and who was a great SA no matter what crime he was investigating was SA Lou Fain. Lou not only worked bank robberies, but he was also on the SWAT team. In addition, he was also a police instructor and taught many local officers various essentials such as crime-scene investigations and other related subjects. But more than anything, he was a true gentleman who worked hard and expected the same out of anyone he worked with.

One day Lou came to me and told me that a subject of one of his bank robberies wanted to surrender, and Lou asked me if I could assist him. It was the policy of the FBI that a minimum of two SAs be present in any arrest situation unless circumstances dictated differently, such as if an agent was in pursuit of a subject, and no other SAs were immediately present.

I told Lou I would be glad to help him and felt honored that this legend would ask me. The car that Lou drove was an ugly yellow station wagon. He drove this large car as he spent a great deal of his time on the road traveling around the state, teaching police officers. He always had loads of equipment and materials to use in his classes, so it was easier to transport everything in this station wagon than a standard-sized sedan.

So I got into the car with Lou, and off we went. He drove to a location in Scottsdale, and, sure enough, our bank-robbery subject was there to surrender himself. Lou placed him under arrest, handcuffed him, and put him in the backseat of the station wagon behind the passenger seat. I sat in the backseat with the subject and sat behind Lou, who was driving.

We were returning eastbound on Van Buren Road heading back to the office, and as we approached a busy intersection, the car ran out of gas. Now, policy dictated that whenever any car dropped below a quarter of a tank of gas, whoever was using the car was responsible for filling it up with gas. Anyone using the car after that would have gas if they were responding to an emergency situation. Since this car was assigned directly to Lou, he was responsible for seeing that it had gas, but apparently being the gentleman he was, he had allowed someone else to use the car while he did paperwork in the office. That person should have filled the car up but did not do so.

It was the middle of summer, and the temperature was at least 110 degrees outside. We were approaching this intersection when the car ran out of gas, and there just happened to be a gas station to our right about a half block ahead. So Lou got out of the car, put the gear in neutral, and started pushing it forward as he held on to the steering wheel and guided it. As he pushed it into the intersection, there was a slight incline, and as he pushed it forward, it came to the slight rise in the street. Just as the car was about to top the rise, the car stopped and started rolling backward—not fast but just enough to get to the bottom of the slight rise, and then it stopped. Lou tried again, and the same thing happened. The car rolled backward again. After several more attempts, it came to a stop, and he looked back at me with a very red face, profusely sweating, and said, "Do you think you could get your ass out and help me push this damned thing?"

The handcuffed subject looked up and said, "Do you want me to help you guys too?"

Lou said, "You sit right there and don't move a muscle!" Lou was adamant, and the subject did not say anything else as he could see that Lou was not very happy.

Now had I considered getting out and helping Lou earlier, but we had the subject in the car, and the last thing I wanted to do was get out to help him and leave the prisoner unsecured in the car. I said, "Sure, let me go to the back, and I'll push, you steer, and we will get there." I went to the back of the car, where it was easier to push, and a citizen walking nearby came over to assist, so we had no problem. Lou steered the car to the gas station and pulled over to a pump to get the gas. The citizen left, and I got back into the car next to our prisoner. He asked me if Lou was very mad, and I just told him not to talk about it.

After Lou got back in the car and got it started, we drove to the office, and Lou just said how hot a day it was and appeared as if nothing had happened. However, I learned from our secretary that Lou got in touch with the person who had used his car earlier and read him the riot act for not putting gas in the car. I am just glad that person was not me; I never wanted to get on his bad side.

As I mentioned, Lou was a real legend in our office, and I do not believe he ever had an enemy. He was loved by everybody and was sorely missed when he later retired. He often told this story about how I watched him try to push a car with two people inside in "140-degree" weather, and we laughed about it for years.

I later had the opportunity to work with his son Mike Fain, who was on the esteemed FBI hostage-rescue team and who later transferred to the Phoenix division. We worked on several cases together, and Mike was just like his dad—give him something to do, and he would work the case unceasingly. He was one hard worker and a great friend.

———◆———

It was about 11:00 p.m. one night, and I woke up to the ringing of the telephone. This was not unusual as the work I and many other SAs did necessitated being called at all hours of the night. We worked reactive work, which meant that as soon as a crime was committed, we reacted immediately, responding to initiate the investigation of the offense.

The call came from our central office, and the FBI employee gave me the telephone number of a police officer who needed to be contacted immediately. This officer worked security at Sky Harbor International Airport in Phoenix. The employee had no further information other than the case involved a passenger of an airline flight.

I immediately called the officer, who advised me that a person had been removed from an airplane that had landed in Phoenix. Apparently, this passenger had interfered with the flight crew; this was a federal offense, and the officer was notifying the FBI of what transpired.

I asked what the passenger had done, and the officer said that he approached the lavatory while the airplane was in flight, but someone was already in the lavatory. He knocked on the door, and the flight attendant told him to be a bit patient and that it would only be a moment or so, and then he could use the lavatory. He did not want to wait, became belligerent, and started yelling that he wanted in immediately. When he realized that being obnoxious was doing no good, he reached down, pulled his zipper down, and urinated in the aisle of the airplane.

The flight attendant told the pilot what this passenger had done, so he sent a male officer to assist the flight attendant as the passenger was getting out of hand. They convinced him to be seated, and since he no longer needed the lavatory, he complied. The pilot diverted the Los Angeles–bound aircraft to land in Phoenix, and the airport police were notified. When the plane landed, the person was removed from the airplane and arrested.

The officer further advised that the person arrested was one of the leading members of a very famous current rock group who felt that everyone should comply with his demands. He was intoxicated and very upset that he had been arrested.

The officer asked if the FBI wanted to assume jurisdiction, and I told him I would presume we would accept it but wanted to make a call to the AUSA to get authorization before I committed myself. I would get right back to him.

I called an AUSA whom I always worked with and provided him with this information, and he immediately authorized federal prosecution. I recontacted the police officer and told him we would assume jurisdiction. He said he had a report on this incident, but the plane had already departed, so there were no witnesses to interview at this time. The officer had, however, taken the names of all relevant witnesses and information on how to contact them for future interviews. He did an outstanding job, and as a result, it was not necessary to leave home to conduct the investigation at this time. The officer said that he would have the prisoner transferred downtown to the Maricopa County jail, and he would have a "hold for FBI" notification placed on this prisoner at the jail. I thanked him and went back to bed.

The next morning after arriving at the office, I pulled the information that had been generated by the night employee and put together a federal complaint form. This form contained relevant information that would later be reviewed and approved by the AUSA who authorized the filing of the complaint with a US magistrate. All proper documentation would be completed for this matter.

I contacted the SA who had the case assigned to him and told him what I had done so far. Together we worked to complete all the necessary paperwork, so all we had to do was file the complaint and take the prisoner before the US magistrate. This SA was a first-office SA and was a diligent hard worker, so he took the brunt of all the work and efficiently had it completed.

All we needed to do now was go to the jail, pick this prisoner up, and take him to the united marshal's office at the federal building, where they would hold him in their lockup for us. We would then talk to the AUSA for the approval he had given the night before with any additional information we might have generated and file the necessary paperwork with the US magistrate. The US magistrate would then issue an arrest warrant for the prisoner, although the prisoner was already in custody. This was a procedure that we had to adhere. We then would take the prisoner before the US magistrate for an initial appearance. The prisoner would be told what charges were pending, be given an attorney if he could not afford one, and determine if he could be released on bail. If so, a bail amount would be set.

We went down to the Maricopa County jail to get this prisoner. When we entered, we went to the interior of the facility where all the prisoners were being held and contacted the officer on duty. We gave him the name of the inmate, so the officer checked the records and found the "hold for FBI" notification for this person. He then went and retrieved him.

After a few moments, the officer returned with this person, and, sure enough, he was one of the leading members of this famous rock group and was easily recognizable. As he approached us, he came forward to shake our hands. He thanked us for coming to get him and said the FBI was trying to screw him over with some "BS charges."

Apparently, when he had arrived at the jail and been booked into the facility, he had asked for a telephone call and placed a collect call to his agent in Los Angeles, advising what had happened and saying that he needed an attorney right away to represent him. So upon seeing us arrive in suits, he assumed we were his lawyers. He kept rambling on, and we just let him keep talking. We did not have any reason, nor were we mandated, to advise him we were not his attorneys. He said that all he did was piss in the aisle of the airplane, and the flight attendant became very upset and was making a big deal out of all this. Easiest confession I ever had.

Once he finished rambling on, I then advised him we were with the FBI as we put handcuffs on him for our transport to the federal building. He became silent, and his eyes were bulging out once he realized we were not his attorneys. We took him out of the jail facility, put him in our car, and took him to the Federal Building. Once in the car, he started joking with us, saying that he was not a bad guy, and he did not hate the FBI or feel they were trying to screw him around. I told him not to worry about it, but we did have his voluntary statement that he had earlier blurted out, and he just shook his head.

We later met up with his attorney, who came to represent him before the US magistrate. This lawyer was quite pleasant and asked us if we had interviewed his client. I said just briefly after he blurted out to us what happened and that was to just clarify a few issues. The attorney just laughed and stated that he would get bail posted for him and see if his client could return to California, where he lived and performed on stage.

This matter took a while to settle as the performer was allowed to enter a plea without returning to Arizona. I cannot recall what the ultimate disposition was in this case other than I understand that one of the things he had to do was write an apology letter to the airline's crew. I researched this further to see if anything additional was done but could find nothing.

———

Working for the FBI is a very gratifying job that does not seem like work because it is so enjoyable. However, it is a very demanding occupation that can drain you if you allow it. So whenever the time arises, it is always good to take some time away and spend it with the family. This was my experience one year.

We planned a vacation to take our sons to Disneyland in Anaheim, California. I had been there on several occasions when I was younger, enjoyed it immensely, and knew our boys would love it. They were old enough to enjoy the park, and sometimes we'd even allow them to go on their own around the park and not be watched over by nagging parents. So off they went with Rosie and me following at a discreet distance. We might appear to be very trusting, but we still are not very dumb. I knew my sons.

We left for Disneyland on Sunday and planned to spend three days there. We would then leave on Thursday morning, drive to San Diego, and visit SeaWorld on Friday. I had never been to SeaWorld but had heard so much about it and always wanted to see the performing orcas and other fish and events they held.

We arrived in Anaheim on Sunday evening and, as planned, visited Disneyland for three solid days. We took our time, visited everything, and took many rides, several times on the favorite ones.

On Thursday morning, we left Anaheim for the drive to San Diego, which was not too far down the line. We arrived at our hotel, which was on the ocean, and settled in the room. The boys went down to the beach while Rosie and I stayed in the room and from the balcony had an outstanding view of the Pacific Ocean as far as the eye could see. We looked down and watched the boys playing on the beach and going into the ocean, just having a ball. I sat on the balcony with a mixed drink enjoying the great weather, the view, and my family. Life was great and was getting better.

Just then the telephone rang. Uh-oh, I thought. Who knows I'm here? Must be the office downstairs, or my neighbor back in Phoenix telling me my house just burned down, or the office. Must be the office downstairs.

Rosie answered and, after a moment, told me that Doug Hopkins, an SA in the Phoenix division and a good friend, needed to talk to me. As I answered, Doug asked how things were going, and I said things were great. He asked when I was returning to Phoenix, and I said we were coming back on Saturday, and I would be back in the office on Monday.

Doug said things had changed. I asked him what he meant. He stated that he had a bank-robbery case that was currently in trial and that I needed to testify in this case on Friday—the next day. I asked him if he was joking, and he said no. I asked if anyone else could testify, but he said my testimony was related to some evidence I had located at the crime scene, and I was the only one who could testify to it. I then asked if this could wait until Monday. He said he knew I was on vacation, and he had relayed this to the AUSA prosecuting the case for the government. The AUSA had presented the dilemma to the federal judge in this case, and if a recess could be taken until Monday, I would be back to testify. The judge responded that justice waits for no one and that I'd be summoned to testify, or the evidence would not be allowed. So there was no option but having me return to Phoenix the following day. Doug apologized, but that did not make it any easier.

On Friday morning, Rosie and the boys took me to the airport for the flight to Phoenix, and she told me she would take the boys to SeaWorld that day. I flew to Phoenix, and Doug had an SA pick me up at the airport, drive me home to put on a suit, and drive me to the federal building. Arriving there, I went up to the courtroom, and as I entered, the AUSA advised the judge that the witness had arrived and was prepared to testify. I then went up to the witness chair, where I was sworn in, gave my name, and waited. The judge thanked me for coming in and asked how my vacation was going. I just smiled and said that we'd had a good time. He then told the AUSA to proceed.

The AUSA handed me a piece of evidence that I looked at and identified as evidence I had located and secured. I had the date and my initials on it for identification. The AUSA asked that the evidence be entered into evidence, and this was done. The prosecution said it had no further questions, and the defense was allowed to ask any questions but stated that they had none. The judge excused me and asked the AUSA if I was needed any longer; having been told that I was not, he advised me that I was excused and did not need to return to the courtroom.

I entered the courtroom, was sworn in, gave my testimony, and finished in a total time of about ten minutes at the most. As I was leaving, Doug winked at me, thanked me, and told me to get back to San Diego.

So the SA who had brought me to the courthouse and was waiting for me took me home to change out of my suit and took me back to the airport for my return flight to San Diego. Fortunately, it was only a one-hour flight, but by the time I got there, the day was about over. Rosie and the boys picked me up at the airport, and she looked like she had been run over by a bus. She looked at me through threatening eyes and said that we would never go on another vacation as long as we lived if I was still working for the FBI.

Just imagine having four boys, aged thirteen, twelve, and ten (the twins) wanting to do everything all at once, and not having Dad around. She did not want them to run around and have the leeway they had at Disneyland, so she stayed with them all day long, and they ran her ragged. Of course, I looked at them with those angelic looks on their faces and thought that Mom was exaggerating. I knew better, but now that it was over, nothing could be done.

She asked me how the trial was going, and I told her how long I had spent on the witness stand and had a smirk on my face. She did not laugh. Neither did I.

So I decided to make it up to her and told Rosie and the boys that we were going to a very nice restaurant and not having fast-food hamburgers that night. We heard about a really nice seafood restaurant, so we made reservations and went there for the evening to eat. Of course, the boys were not too happy with fish, but after what they had put their mother through that day, they decided not to push it and ordered something they found and acted like it was good. Of course, Rosie now believed I owed her big and ordered a lobster and steak. I decided not to argue over the cost of these ugly crustaceans and let her enjoy the evening. She did, and I paid the price.

The next day, we got up, had an excellent breakfast, and drove the six hours back to Phoenix. It would be years later before I was able to see SeaWorld for the first time. And this later trip happened after I retired from the FBI.

I must admit that this was not unusual in this line of work. There was one incident when the SA was on a fishing trip in Colorado and had to return to his office as his presence was needed for something imperative.

The SA from the nearest office was dispatched to where the SA said he was going on vacation and, arriving there, found out the SA was with a fishing guide out on a huge lake. The dispatched SA secured a boat and went out on the lake to find the SA in question. Having found him, he advised the agent he was needed back at his office and should call the office. It was a good thing the dispatched SA was in another boat, and the SA could not walk on water (although some of them thought they could). Otherwise, there could have been a problem. The agent returned with his guide, got on a phone, and called home. He learned he was needed on an important case and had to leave his fishing trip. I heard he was unhappy, but there was not too much he could do about it. Justice waits for no one.

———

I have a good friend named Tommy, who told me a story that he found to be quite hilarious but expounded on the importance of being an FBI agent and the image one projects.

He was working in a large office one day, starting very early. He was working fugitives, and the early-morning hours were the best time to locate and arrest fugitives. He and the other SAs were extremely busy all day long. At about 6:00 p.m., he and several other SAs decided to have a drink before taking a subway home for the evening.

So they went to their favorite watering hole and had a drink, and as the second one was being ordered, one of the other SAs told Tommy he had just talked to a source and learned that a fugitive he was looking for might have been located. So Tommy canceled his second drink for both of them, and they both went to the location where the fugitive might be. They did a cursory check at some apartments but were not sure if the person was there. The person they were looking for was a military deserter, and on many occasions, all one had to do was to let family members know that if the individual turned him- or herself in, they would return the individual to the military and be done with it.

So both of them went to the door and knocked, and a small black lady about seventy years old answered the door. They asked her for the subject by name, and she said that person was her grandson, but he was not at her home at this time. She invited them in and asked them if they wanted any coffee or tea, and they said they didn't.

They spoke with her for a few minutes, getting some information about her grandson, and asked her if she had a better photo of him. The one they had was dated and faded out. She said she would look around and got up to leave the room.

As Tommy told me, he and his buddy sat there for a while, and then Tommy said he jerked up, and there was this lady sitting in her rocking chair, holding on to a photograph. He looked over at his buddy, and he was fast asleep with his head resting on the back of the couch. Tommy looked at his wristwatch and noted it was about 9:00 p.m. He woke his buddy up and whispered to him that it was nine. His partner looked stunned and looked at his watch. Sure enough, 9:00 p.m.

Tommy and his buddy had fallen asleep waiting for this kind lady to retrieve a photo and had slept for about an hour or so. The lady was just patiently sitting there waiting for them to wake up. When they did awaken, they looked at her, and she merely handed them the picture of her grandson.

Tommy asked her why she did not wake them up, and she said they looked tired and because they were the FBI, they could sleep whenever they wanted. Tommy did not try to explain anything to her as he just wanted to get out of there. He asked her to have her grandson call him the next day, and they would help him get back to the military.

It was not the next day, but within several days, Tom received a call from the fugitive deserter. He reminded them that they had been at his grandmother's house several days earlier and had fallen asleep. He now was ready to turn himself in. Tommy and his buddy went back to the grandmother's house, found him, and arrested him, telling him this was strictly procedure and they would just turn him over to the military, who would deal with him. They saw the grandmother one last time; she asked them if they were rested up, and they assured her they were.

———◆———

One of the most beloved directors the FBI ever had was Director Clarence M. Kelley. Director Kelley enjoyed a very successful career in the FBI, retiring in 1961 after having served in many leadership roles in the FBI hierarchy. After this retirement, he served as chief of police for the Kansas City, Missouri, Police Department

In 1973, Director Kelley was nominated as the FBI director by President Richard M. Nixon with immediate confirmation by Congress. Every SA I ever knew had only praise for this fine man.

On one occasion, he and his wife traveled to Phoenix, where he was to deliver a speech. As is the case whenever an FBI director is in travel status, he had a team of bodyguards who called upon SAs from the field division where the director would be going. These SAs assisted on the protection detail by providing vehicles and drivers as they knew the community and where hospitals and other emergency facilities were located.

On this occasion, I happened to be selected to assist on this detail. I had served on other details, but this one stands out as remarkable because of this great man.

Director Kelley and his entourage were staying at a very nice facility in Scottsdale. During this occasion, some professional football players, both active and retired, were also staying at this facility and were playing in a charitable golf tournament. Director Kelley was not playing in the golf tournament, and many professional athletes had the opportunity to meet this director during his stay.

Another SA who worked this detail was SA Douglas Hopkins. Doug and I, along with other SAs, maintained surveillance on the facility where the director and his wife were staying and drove them anywhere they needed to go. We put in many hours over that weekend.

On Saturday evening, the director and his wife were to attend a function at the home of the Phoenix SAC. As they were leaving their accommodations, Doug pulled the car they would be riding in to the front door, and they started entering the vehicle along with several other protection-detail SAs. I was driving a secondary car following their vehicle, so if there were a vehicle breakdown, we would have immediate assistance by having the second vehicle. As they were entering the car Doug was driving, I noticed that Director Kelley came over to the driver's-side window and spoke to Doug. He then started walking back to my vehicle, and I began to get out of the car to see what the problem was. He just motioned me not to get out, so I rolled the window down. He asked me if anyone was riding with me. I told him that I was alone and just driving the backup car. He then asked if he could ride with me, and I said absolutely. Was I going to tell him no?

I started to get out to open up the passenger door as he went around, and he said not to bother as he could do it himself. He then got into the car. I radioed to Doug that my passenger was ready, and Doug started driving with me following behind.

This man was just incredible. He thanked Doug and me for taking the time to make sure he and his wife were having a great and safe trip to Phoenix. He then asked me if I could be honest with him about something. I told him that I would be happy to give him an honest opinion if that was what he was seeking. He just asked if the SAs on the street thought he was doing a good job as director or if there were any weaknesses he had that needed to be addressed. He wanted an honest opinion as he was insisting that FBI SAs were important to him. I was frank with him and told him we were extremely pleased with his performance to date and always looked forward to better times. I expressed the appreciation of the SAs in our division by noting that the new vehicles we were getting all had air conditioning in them. In the past, many new vehicles did not have the air conditioning because of the associated expense. He laughed at that and said that he would make sure the SAC knew that all cars in the Phoenix division and other areas of the country with extreme heat conditions also had air conditioning in their cars.

The trip to this function took about twenty minutes' driving time, and Director Kelley and I just talked like we were old friends. As we arrived at the home of the SAC, he asked me if Doug and I would be available the next day, and I said we would be. He asked if we could pick him and his wife up at around 9:00 a.m. and take them to Carefree, Arizona, as they wanted to have lunch there and perhaps look at some real estate for when he retired as director. I said we could make sure that happened.

We left them off at this house, and we were informed that we could terminate for the night, and another group of SAs would take them back to their accommodations in Scottsdale. I told Doug about the director's request, and he said he would meet me in the morning in Scottsdale.

Precisely at 9:00 a.m., Doug and I pulled up in our car at the resort, and the director and his wife left their accommodations and entered our car. Doug drove as we went north to Carefree and Cave Creek and drove around the area, showing the director some locations he might be interested in. We then stopped for lunch at a very busy restaurant. I went in and asked for a table for four and was told that it might take about ten minutes or so. Within minutes, we were seated and had a very nice lunch. This was incredible. I had been around other dignitaries who made you feel like they were special and needed to be tended to at every minute. Not Director Kelley and his wife. They were very down to earth, and talking with them was like conversing with old friends. We talked about families and growing up, and it was just one great time we had. No business talk on this day. Just a day of relaxation and fun.

When the check came, Director Kelley reached for it and said the meal was on him. Doug and I had already agreed that we would pick up the check. How many people can say they bought lunch for the FBI director and his wife? Well, Doug and I can say that.

In the early afternoon, we returned them to their room, and we were allowed to go off duty for the remainder of the day. The following morning, we drove them to the FBI office, where Director Kelley met and greeted the office personnel and gave a small talk to all the employees. We then took them to the airport to the FBI private jet that would return them to Washington, DC. I gave Mrs. Kelley a copy of the *Tombstone Epitaph* newspaper that I had purchased one time through my travels in southern Arizona. She was delighted and thanked me. About a week later,

I received a thank-you card signed by her for the small gift and the grand time she said she had. Also, Director Kelley sent me a large autographed photograph of himself as director.

Over the years, I was called upon four additional times to assist when other directors came into the division for some official business. Just about every one of them was personal and pleasant, some more friendly than others, but that is to be expected. They had a lot on their minds, and travel was a necessary evil to maintain a high level of cooperation with other state and federal agencies. But the weekend with Director Kelley was one weekend that will never be forgotten.

Author with FBI Director Clarence M. Kelley

Arriving at the FBI office about 4:30 a.m., I started a coffee pot for some hot coffee to drink as I prepared some reports. I went into the lavatory that was located just outside the elevator doors and the main entrance to the FBI work space. Upon entering this lavatory, I noticed a small red-and-white, six-pack cooler on top of the towel dispenser and recognized it as the lunch box of one of our FBI agents. He apparently had brought it into the restroom prior to leaving the previous night and inadvertently left it there. I thought of taking it to his desk, which was on another floor, but then thought he might recall leaving it in the restroom and come to get it when he came to the office that morning. So I just left it and subsequently returned to my desk, finished my report, and left the office at about 7:30 a.m. for an appointment with a witness to one of my cases.

I returned to the office at about 9:00 a.m. and upon arriving, noticed a large number of employees standing outside of the building with police cars and fire trucks surrounding the building. I parked my car and walked over toward the building where everyone was milling around. I saw SA Bob Seymour talking to a few detectives from the Phoenix PD who I also knew. I walked over and asked what was going on. These detectives, great people and outstanding investigators, were assigned to a unit that worked bombing cases. Bob was the FBI bomb technician and said that we had a bomb scare at the office. I asked if someone had called in the scare. Bob said no and that a possible explosive device had been found in the building by a clerical employee who then notified the FBI administration. The building was cleared, and the bomb detail of the Phoenix PD responded. They subsequently entered the building, found the device, and determined it was not a bomb. At this time, employees were starting to enter the building to return to work.

Wow, I thought and asked where the device was located. Bob said that it was in the men's lavatory and described it as a small red-and-white box, from what he understood. I thought back to that morning and said, "Hell, that's not a bomb. That's a lunch box that belongs to one of the agents." Bob just shook his head and asked me how I knew what it was since nobody but the Phoenix PD bomb detail had seen the box. I told him that I saw that box earlier that morning and recognized it as being a lunch box. Bob did not believe me and thought I was making up a story. So I told him that not only did I see this box, but I could tell him what was inside of it. I said there was an apple and two cookies, and as I said that, one of the detectives looked at Bob, smiled, and shook his head, confirming that these items were in that box.

Bob is one great guy, so I decided to play this to the hilt. Bob asked me why, when I had seen it, I did not consider that it could be a bomb. I said that was the first thing that entered my mind, so I did what any other SA would do—picked up the box and shook it to see if it exploded. If it did not detonate, it was probably not a bomb, so I opened it and saw the two cookies and the apple and put the lunch box back on the dispenser. Then I shook my head as if in disbelief that the bomb detail was called out on a lunch box. Of course, this story of me believing it might be a bomb and shaking it was made up on the spot to get Bob's reaction.

I then looked at the two detectives, who had smiles on their faces, and told them the next time they were called to come to our office, to call me first and I would go look at the device and determine if they were needed. Bob was shaking his head back and forth, smiling but wondering how I could be so stupid. Bob was one great SA who went to the FBI bombing school, so naturally he was quite taken aback that I would not have considered the ramifications if this were to be a bomb. He was correct since many bombings were occurring throughout the country, and the FBI was being targeted in many cases. I knew it wasn't the first time I had seen it.

Nevertheless, I could not let this opportunity go by without harassing him a bit. I then told Bob that I had not attended the bomb school but was still able to ascertain if something was a bomb or not. I asked him if he had any questions that I could answer for him, and he just looked at me like I was a real idiot.

Over the next couple of weeks, I would pass by Bob, and he would just look at me and shake his head in disbelief. I continued to ask him if he had come across any bombs recently, and he just shook his head. We had a good laugh over this.

In hindsight, Bob was the expert there and correctly did what needed to be done: have bomb experts locate the device and determine if it was real or not. What he did not need was some smart ass to come along and not only tell him it was not a bomb but what the box contained: two cookies and an apple.

The next time I see Bob, I will just look him in the eye and say those famous words to him to see if he recalls this incident: "two cookies and an apple."

———

I was contacted by a robbery detective from the PXPD who said that some small markets were being robbed at gunpoint by a lone Hispanic female. She was getting several hundreds of dollars during each robbery, but because she was not getting much money, she was robbing more and more of these markets. He had some surveillance still photos of her that were not of good quality as she had most of her face covered. He wanted to know if I could take these photos and contact all of our informants to see if they might be able to identify her. She was getting more and more violent and appeared to be on drugs, so he needed to arrest her before she harmed or even killed someone.

We checked with our sources with no results. However, after several days, the detective called me and told me to discontinue as the robber had turned herself in to the police.

He said that the police department had decided to stage a crime scene from her last robbery and put the video on television. They got their actors together and reenacted the robbery, showing the female running out of the store with her red bandana over her face and wearing the brown jacket with the gun in her right hand. Again, this was merely a reenactment of the robbery.

The robber was watching TV that evening, saw the reenactment, and decided that since the police had her on camera, she'd better surrender and hope they would go easy on her. So she surrendered and admitted to all the robberies she had committed. She did not realize this was only a reenactment and not an actual video of her committing the robbery.

I'd never seen a happier detective, who said he wished all robbers were this dumb.

———◆———

One of my best friends in the Phoenix division was SA Douglas Hopkins. Doug and I worked bank robberies together and helped each other out as much as we could. Doug was fun to work with, and we just enjoyed each other's company while working together.

One day he received a radio call from SA Mike Roof, who said he and SA Jack Loughery had a fugitive located and wanted to know if Doug and

I could come out to help him and Jack by covering the back as they went through the front door to arrest the fugitive. Doug said we would be there shortly after getting the address from Mike.

This location was in Glendale, just west of Phoenix. As we drove along Glendale Avenue about four miles from our destination, we ran into heavy traffic. Doug changed lanes, and, for some reason, the driver in the car behind Doug in the lane he entered became upset and started honking. Doug just ignored him and, in another moment, changed back to the first lane. The person behind Doug followed him into that lane and kept honking his horn. Then the person returned to the original lane and, as he pulled alongside Doug, started yelling. In fact, there were four young men in this car, and as they were all yelling; they were also flipping Doug off.

Doug said that if we were not in such a hurry to help Mike and Jack, he would stop these idiots and read them the riot act. They kept yelling, so Doug just looked at me, smiled, and said that Mike and Jack would just have to wait a few minutes longer.

He then pulled behind the car, which had bumper stickers that indicated these four young men might be students at a local trade school. He turned on his siren and put up the red light, and several of these young men turned around with bulging eyes. They probably figured they must have been idiots by flipping off and yelling at law-enforcement officers. Doug just said that he would take the driver, and I should take the other three. Huh? I get three, and he gets one? Thanks, Doug.

I got out of the car and approached the passenger side of their car, telling them just to stay in the car and put their hands on the dashboard and backseat. Doug had the driver step out of the car, and he was reading him the riot act. I could not hear what he was saying as the passengers were apologizing and making excuses. I just told them they were acting like real idiots, and they were fortunate they did it to us rather than someone else who might take exception to what they were doing. By the time Doug was finished with the driver, I saw Doug shake his hand and tell him to get back in the car and use better judgment in the future. As we were leaving, I looked back, and all of them were smiling and waving good-bye. Maybe they learned a lesson that day—and then again, maybe not.

On another occasion, Doug and I were eating lunch at a restaurant adjacent to a shopping-mall area. We had a portable radio with us, and a bank robbery alert came out advising us of a bank robbery in progress. We were just about done eating and got up to leave. As we walked back to our car, we saw a school bus from another Arizona city parked in the parking lot. What drew our attention to this bus were the yelling and loud and obnoxious noises coming from the young men inside it. We noticed that an elderly lady was walking near the bus, and several of the young lads started yelling at her and using foul language. She was doing nothing but walking with a small package in her hand and walking with a cane. One youngster in particular was screaming with his head out the window and being a total jerk.

I took exception to this, but Doug was furious. We walked over to the bus, and this generated more verbal abuse from these young men. Apparently, they were in town for a football game and were just letting off steam, but what they were doing was uncalled for. Doug walked over to the elderly lady to make sure she was OK, and she said she was. Doug then walked over to the lad who had his head out the window to talk to him. The young men told Doug where to go, and this remark caused some of the others in the bus to start jeering at Doug and me. Doug then pulled out his credentials, and the bus went silent. We could hear some of them laughing at the person who was now pulling his head back in the bus and closing his window. Doug was yelling at him to open his window so he could talk to him, but he refused.

Just then a man came toward us from a nearby business and wanted to know what was going on. He was the coach of this football team and thought that Doug and I were harassing his players. Doug explained to him what we had observed these players doing and specifically pointed to the lad sitting at the window that was just closed.

We identified ourselves to this coach, who was furious—not at us but at his team. He thanked us and shook our hands and said that he would make sure these young men were disciplined for their inappropriate actions.

We left, and as we got to our car and looked back at the bus, we could see the coach stomping up and down the aisle, yelling at his players.

I am confident these young men learned a lesson that day. But then again, maybe not.

———◆———

One great employee whom I remain good friends with to this day was one of our radio technicians named Fred Taylor. Fred is one fun-loving guy who loves to tell a good joke and just enjoy the company he is with. Every time I see Fred, he always starts off with, "Hey, I have a great joke for you. Did you hear the one about..."

Fred and a few other technicians were responsible for all the radio-communication equipment in the Phoenix division. This meant that the entire state of Arizona had to be covered by these men so that our radio transmissions would operate properly anywhere in the state. There might be a few dead areas where there would be no radio reception, but for the most part, it was their responsibility to ensure that we always had communications whenever we needed assistance or information of some sort. Our lives depended on their dedication to making sure all the communication gear was in tip-top shape.

These technicians were always checking and double-checking equipment to ensure that our radios were operated properly. But like anything else, because it was electronic equipment, it was always subject to problems.

There was one month in particular when it seemed that whenever I needed to speak on my portable radio, it would go dead and not operate. I took the radio to Fred, and he examined it, telling me it appeared it was functioning properly. However, to appease me, he made some battery changes and performed some other things to increase the dependability of the radio. It worked fine for several days, and then it acted up again.

Back to Fred it went. Although we were friends, he would see me coming and shake his head as he knew I was getting a bit irritated with this portable radio. He checked it again and said it appeared to be fine but again but did a few things to it, and as I left, the radio was working. I told him that we had an important surveillance later on in the evening, and it was essential that the radio was operating properly. He just said it was working now and asked me if I had any other suggestions. Of course I didn't since I knew it was working.

Later that evening before the surveillance, and being a bit paranoid about this radio, I tested it with the office, and they advised they could read me loud and clear. I also tested it on a car radio, and it was clear. I was still uncomfortable as the problems kept presenting themselves at the most inopportune times.

As we started the surveillance, I was out on foot and was to report the movements of several subjects from the top of a hill. We could not park a car in the area, so I had to be on foot. As I moved to my location, I tested the radio again, and it worked fine. Once in position, I asked the cars if they could read my transmissions, and there were no problems. Every ten minutes or so, I did a minor radio check, and the cars came back with, "Loud and clear."

The surveillance was silent for about an hour or so, and then I noticed movement by the targeted subjects, so I radioed out what was happening. Nothing. No response from any car or the office. I tried to reach them again and still nothing. The subjects were getting into a car to leave, and I needed to alert our other units of their movement, but the radio was not functioning. I tried again—still nothing. Now I was really upset, so I just stood up, yelled out to the FBI cars parked below the hill, and said the subjects were moving away from the house in their car. So much for being discreet.

They could not understand why I was doing this instead of telling them through the radio.

One of the SAs transmitted to me and asked me to talk back to him. I heard this transmission loud and clear. I then talked back to him, and he heard me loud and clear. So I now transmitted to him the fact that the subjects were on the move, and our other cars picked them up, and the moving surveillance continued.

What was going on with my radio? It worked whenever I tested it, but when I really needed it, it did not work. This was driving me nuts.

The next day, I gave the radio a transmission check, and it did not function. I tried it again, and it again did not function. Good. I would take this right over to Fred and show him. Fortunately, he was in the office and not at the radio shop where he spent most of his time, so I only had to go upstairs and find him in the radio room talking with Kelly, our daytime radio dispatcher. He saw me coming and smiled at me. I asked him to take a look at the radio, so he talked into it, and it worked fine. He asked me what was wrong with it. I took it and talked into it, and it worked fine.

Fred then asked me to sit down. I thought he might be pulling a joke on me but also knew that he would not do anything to jeopardize any surveillance. So I sat down, and he asked me if I knew how to operate the radio. He asked me if I knew that I had to depress the transmit button to talk and release it to hear. I told him I knew all this, but I looked over at Kelly, who was laughing at his sarcastic way of trying to teach an SA the proper way of transmitting on a radio. He then became serious and said he did not know what was wrong with the radio, but he would check the radio out again.

Later that day, he came over to me with a new radio and said this new one was being charged out to me. He was taking the older radio and would try to find out what was causing the problems. He said this radio was just unreliable and unpredictable, and he was removing it from service. He ran some tests on it, and all were fine, but he did not want any SA to be out working with a radio that was not dependable. He did not know what the problem was, could not fix it, and commented that occasionally things like this happened.

Once I got the new radio, I never again had any more trouble with it.

While mentioning Fred, there was the time when he was assisting SA Al Zumpf and several other SAs in northern Arizona on a moving surveillance. Some cars were stopped by traffic signals, and others were stopped by traffic in general to the point that the targeted subjects who were being followed could not be located. Several cars broke off and went to the east side and the west side of this small town to hopefully find the subjects. Fred and several other units temporarily broke off for a quick pit stop at a local fast-food restaurant to get some food to take with them and to use the restroom.

Fred went into the restroom and walked up to the urinal to use it. As he did, he casually glanced over at the person next to him. He was amazed to see that the person standing there using the adjoining urinal was one of the targeted subjects they had been following. Fred allowed that person to finish, and as he left, Fred also left. He departed the restaurant and spotted the car they had originally been following parked on the opposite side of the parking lot. He then called all the other units to come to his location and continue the surveillance. They did, and the remainder of the surveillance went on like clockwork.

When I later heard about this, I asked Fred if he had washed his hands before he left the restroom. With the quizzical look he always had, he said he could not remember. Then he said he must have as he ate his hamburger as he drove, and it sure tasted good to him.

I believe that what added to the taste of his hamburger was the fact that Fred spotted the target that allowed the case to continue as projected without any further glitches. Good for him—he deserves to be recognized for his observations.

CHAPTER 7

Memories

———

AND SO THAT IS A small compilation of recollections of my personal little world where I spent time daily in the FBI. The many other SAs who preceded me, worked in the same period of time as I did, and followed me have their own stories to tell. Some have done so in other books, and many have chosen to keep their stories in their own minds to share with family and close friends. Many have stories that made world headlines, and then there are the smaller stories that never will make print but will be recalled occasionally by those involved.

It never occurred to me that my life would be filled with episodes of eternally recollected events. Most days just seemed to be routine and uneventful but filled with necessary paperwork to which we were all accustomed. Once the excitement of the chase ended, the work really started, with follow-up investigations, court proceedings, and conclusions to the investigation. In all honesty, I did not care for all this extraneous work, but it was necessary for a successful resolution. I often commented that a perfect world would be two SAs paired up—one who loved the investigations and the chase and one who loved paperwork. But that was not to be and never will.

Every SA who has worked for the FBI has made everlasting friends in all the offices where he or she has been assigned. We are just like those in every other business where people cooperate and become accustomed to the friendships and acquaintances of their colleagues. Special Agents like Bob Prida, Kelly Sanderson, Susan Stamper, Jason Deaton, Jim Cornett, Reno Walker, Ron Myers, Jim Ryan, and Ed Hall have become my very close friends. And of course, there are a hundred others too numerous to mention. Since retiring, I have met many more FBI personnel through social media online. I may or may not meet them in person someday but consider them friends as they are part of the vast FBI family, of which I can say that I am proud to be a member. I correspond daily with many of them and feel as if I have known them my entire life. All I ask is their indulgence and forgiveness if I failed to mention them in this book. It is not that you are forgotten; it is just that select cases were chosen to be written about. I will never forget any of you.

As I now travel down this road of retirement, I have found a different revelation. There is another life outside of the FBI. Having had a great time working for that fine agency, I now can proceed with a different life, anticipating other goals and enjoying what I am doing. I have played golf for years but after taking up artistic painting, I have given that crazy game up. I sing in a community choir named Sounds of the Southwest Singers, with whom I performed at Pearl Harbor and Carnegie Hall and Lincoln Center in New York; backed up Barry Manilow in concert; sang on July 4, 2016, at the Normandy American Cemetery near Omaha Beach in France; and performed on several occasions at Disneyland as well as many, many other venues.

But what are foremost in my memories are all the days of working with the finest group of people one could hope for and recalling all the incidents that I have written about. It was something very few could experience, and I am gratified and thankful that I was afforded this great opportunity.

In closing, I must state that the FBI of today has changed extensively. The personnel all have the same dedication that is expected by the general public, but the work is very different. There has been a dramatic shift toward terrorism, which is as it should be. All it takes is one terrorist to create havoc and huge casualties, and it is the responsibility of the FBI to see this does not happen. They have an extremely difficult job to do, and I am confident they will accomplish what needs to be done to protect all of us in the future. God bless them all, and let us pray that they are successful and are able to go home safely each night, knowing our country is safe in their hands.

Unmitigated Justice

Anthony E. Oldham

Available in paperback from

CreateSpace, Amazon, and

local bookstores.

Turn the page for a preview of the novel

Unmitigated Justice.

Prologue

1996

"Boyd, you are such a lover boy. I know what you're trying to do. We didn't drive up here to see this great view of Tucson and the twinkling of the city lights. Again! You have other things on your mind—and it ain't going to work."

"C'mon, Jennifer, just a kiss or two," Boyd said. "One day soon, we'll be husband and wife, and I know how you'll be—you know—begging me to hold you and kiss you all the time. So why not get a little practice now so that everything will be perfect when that time comes?"

Laughingly, Jennifer said, "Well, maybe a kiss or two but nothing more. Besides, it's getting late, and Daddy will be at the front door, waiting for me to get home. You don't want to see him when he gets mad. Five minutes max, and then we leave, OK?"

And so the first moment of bliss enwrapped this young couple, who were so much in love with expectations of a long, bright, and happy future.

But it was only a very brief moment.

Suddenly, the driver's door of Boyd's cherry-red Corvette jerked open, startling the young couple and causing Jennifer to scream at the attackers as they violently struck out at them. Boyd lunged at this sudden intrusion, only to be hit across the head with a steel bar that caused him to slump forward in his seat, reeling with horrendous pain.

"Want more, big boy?" the attacker yelled. "Just keep it up. I dare you."

Jennifer screamed again as she was pulled from the car by Jerry Harwell, who laughed as he grabbed at her body. She cried as she begged him to leave her alone, only to be answered by her blouse being ripped from her body by Billy Frederick as he started to molest her. She looked at Boyd for help but, seeing him slouched in his seat of the car, realized that she was at the mercy of these animals.

Both men only laughed as they molested her seminude body on the ground next to the car, and Jennifer whimpered after being told to keep quiet or she would be killed. She saw both men with guns pointed at her, so, fearing for her life, she tried to comply with the outrageous demands they were making. One of the men held her arms while the other, behaving like a wild animal, raped her. She could not believe she was having this nightmare, but coming to terms with what was happening, she submitted to these unimaginable atrocities so that she would not be killed.

Just then, she looked up and saw Boyd coming at the man who was holding her arms. The man she loved so much was coming to save her. Boyd was stumbling, blood all over his head, and his attempt to grab the man holding her only resulted in his being shoved at her. The person holding her jumped back and starting shooting. Boyd then fell on top of her, and she felt a burning sensation in her head and lost consciousness.

Both assailants panicked, as they did not expect any gunplay, so they started the car they'd come to steal and drove away at a high rate of speed, leaving the wounded and bloodied couple on the ground, overlooking the bright lights of Tucson on an otherwise calm and uneventful evening.

CHAPTER 1

————◆————

Friday, July 16, 2010

Jerry Harwell sat anxious but bored in the Arizona State Prison detention holding room in Florence, Arizona. He silently awaited the release formality as detention officers processed all the official documents so he could be released back into the community he had been absent from for the past fourteen years. His paranoia surfaced again as he watched some of the officers through a thick plate-glass window. They merely smirked and continued their work.

Harwell knew they were in no hurry to expedite this process, and he was not going to give them any satisfaction by showing his annoyance. He just sat back, puckered his lips, and silently whistled to himself. Soon he would be able to walk out of this godforsaken prison and return to the abysmal life on the outside—horrid, but unequivocally better than that on the inside.

He would be reporting weekly to a parole officer while living at a state-controlled release housing facility. Every move he made would be monitored by other officials, who would just as soon send him back to this prison as tolerate any abuse of the legal system that he was always violating.

Harwell concluded he had to be extra vigilant in not getting caught if he did anything wrong. He knew he could never walk the straight line as his attorneys and relatives expected and wanted him to do. He might try, but he was a criminal, would always be one, and no amount of therapy would change that. Oh, he would give an outward appearance of good behavior so he could eventually walk away from the housing facility. Hopefully, he would extend his parole officer visits to monthly trips. For now, however, all he wanted was to walk out of this prison to a different way of life. He further vowed that once out, he would never return and would rather die fighting anyone who might try to bring him back.

Harwell and his friend Billy Frederick had been convicted of the bru-tal assault of Jennifer Williams and her fiancé, Boyd Rogers, in 1996. Harwell and Frederick tried to steal their car while Boyd and Jennifer were parked overlooking the city of Tucson, Arizona. Both were shot and left for dead, but both survived. Jennifer suffered a traumatic brain injury that left her catatonic, and Boyd was shot in the spine, which left him paralyzed from the neck down with virtually no hope for any type of recovery.

Testimony and evidence discovered by authorities suggested Boyd re-acted to Frederick as he started molesting Jennifer, resulting in Harwell shooting Boyd three times. Two shots entered nonvital areas of his body, but the third shot struck his spine. One of the bullets passed through Boyd and entered Jennifer's head, causing her traumatic brain injury.

Harwell and Frederick then drove from the area in the stolen Corvette and were observed by another couple, who were driving up and heard the gunshots. The police were summoned, and the stolen car was subsequent-ly found parked behind a local diner that was closed for the night, not too far from where the crime had been committed. Barking dogs created a commotion due to the two men running through a nearby trailer park, causing several neighbors to see them enter the trailer where they both lived. Harwell and Frederick were found by police in their trailer and were subsequently arrested for this horrendous assault.

Searches by authorities at this trailer following the arrests found bloodied clothing containing residue that later matched the DNA from the victims. Although both Harwell and Frederick initially denied any involvement in the crimes, the evidence was overwhelming, and each agreed to plead guilty to being a felon in possession of a weapon, grand theft auto, and two counts of aggravated assault. Both Harwell and Frederick agreed to these pleas rather than going to trial with additional charges of attempted murder being included.

The judge accepted the pleas of both men and sentenced them each to twenty years' incarceration at the Arizona State Prison with the possibility of parole. The judge surmised that the aggravated nature of the assault of the victims came about because of Boyd's aggressiveness in protecting his fiancé, which, although understood, nevertheless contributed to their substantial injuries.

Some fourteen years later, prison overcrowding led to court decisions that mandated some correctional facilities to release prisoners before the completion of their terms. The American Civil Liberties Union was suing various states where the overcrowding conditions occurred. It was the contention of the ACLU and other pro-inmate groups that this excessive overcrowding amounted to cruel and unusual punishment of those convicted. Rather than fight these charges in courts, states started capitulating and settling with these organizations instead of paying the millions of dollars in court costs and attorney fees when the resultant verdict was a toss-up. The states agreed to start releasing prisoners en masse. Federal judges monitored this release policy and would sanction any state that failed to comply with these directed orders from the federal court.

Jerry Harwell was considered for immediate release because of his satisfactory behavior with very few indiscretions while serving his sentence, and therefore, after serving only a little more than fourteen years, he was now being released. Bill Frederick had been involved in several confrontations with other inmates and, because of these major infractions, was not considered for early release.

Back at the prison holding room, Harwell was now called forward, signed his release forms, was handed fifty dollars in cash, and went outside to a waiting van that would transport him to his new residence and life in Phoenix, Arizona. As he entered the van, he wryly smiled as he looked back at the prison walls and lifted up his middle finger as a final good-bye gesture. He had served fourteen years, four months, three weeks, and six days out of his twenty-year sentence for the brutal assault of a young couple who would never be able to enjoy the loving relationship they'd envisioned before that fateful night in 1996.